Amy Liz Harrison

ETERNALLY EXPECTING

PRAISE FOR ETERNALLY EXPECTING

"When I first got sober *Eternally Expecting* is exactly the kind of book I needed. Only another mom in recovery understands the struggles of raising small kids while your life is spiraling. Amy's story is an honest, relatable and totally hilarious look at how wine culture destroys and sobriety rebuilds today's moms."

EMILY LYNN PAULSON, AUTHOR
OF *HIGHLIGHT REAL*, FOUNDER OF SOBER
MOM SQUAD

"Amy Harrison has written a unique and meaningful story or real LIFE. Her tasks as wife, Mother of eight AND recovery from the disease of alcoholism is inspiring. Frankly, I am not sure how she survived these overwhelming challenges. Her journey is an inspiration to all who face such obstacles. This book is profound how Amy relates Motherhood to Recovery, this has probably never been done before. When finished with the book you just want find her, congratulate her and give her a big hug. She has, honestly, accomplished the impossible. As an added incentive, this book is also very well written, and a joy to read. Kudos to Amy, her Husband and wonderful family."

JOHN HENRY BROWNE, ATTORNEY AND
AUTHOR OF *DEVILS DEFENDER* A BEST
NON-FICTION PICK BY AMAZON

"What a story! This book reads like a novel, except that it isn't—it's a gut-wrenchingly honest memoir of the road to recovery. These pages provide encouragement and insight. You're not alone in facing your demons. Thanks for your transparency, Amy."

BILL BUTTERWORTH, AWARD-WINNING
AUTHOR AND SPEAKER

"*Eternally Expecting* reveals the most raw and private moments of a mom struggling to stay afloat while drinking. A decade after her successful fight for freedom from alcoholism, Amy's life has completely transformed. Today, she experiences a healed marriage, genuine connections with her children, true friendships, and joyful laughter... achieved by putting her mental health first. The bi products of her battle were a fulfilling sobriety... and 4 bonus babies housed in her once-retired uterus. An authentic and compelling true story, peppered with laugh-out-loud moments."

SHARON WITT, AUSTRALIAN BEST SELLING
AUTHOR, EDUCATOR AND SPEAKER

ETERNALLY EXPECTING

A MOM OF EIGHT GETS SOBER AND GIVES
BIRTH TO A WHOLE NEW LIFE...HER OWN

AMY LIZ HARRISON

LAUNCH PAD PUBLISHING

Copyright © 2021 by Amy Liz Harrison

All rights reserved.

No part of this book may be reproduced in any form or by any electronic or mechanical means, including information storage and retrieval systems, without written permission from the author, except for the use of brief quotations in a book review.

ISBN: 978-1-951407-54-4 (paperback)

ISBN: 978-1-951407-53-7 (ebook)

DISCLAIMER

This work is non-fiction and, as such, reflects the author's memory of her experiences (which at times, is shaky at best). Many of the names and identifying characteristics of the individuals featured in this book have been changed to protect their privacy, and certain individuals are composites. Exact dialogue and accuracy of some events have been recreated to show the idea of what happened, from the author's perspective. In some cases, conversations have been edited or slightly altered to convey their substance rather than written exactly as they occurred. Most importantly, the author reminds you this is a portrayal of her past, which affected her children, her husband and others. In exchange for her candor, she humbly asks for your gentleness and restraint from judgment.

Gratefully,
  Amy Liz Harrison

To my eight babies, who I carried and delivered, and the husband who gave them to me.
I'm truly powerless over my love for you guys.

CONTENTS

INTRODUCTION

In your hands is the story of my life thus far dear reader. In a way I feel like I'm handing you my newborn baby, so here it is! Be gentle please! You should know that my working title was *Recovery, Unity and Cervix* (a play on the word "Service"), and I'd like to explain it. If you and I were building a house, this introduction would be like the foundation and framework. Chapter one begins with the fun stuff like design elements, paint colors and all the accoutrements. Just bear with me as I take a minute to roll out the blueprints!

The theme of this book is honoring the two most significant events of my life so far: building a family with my husband and my journey back from the depths of alcoholism. As the mother of eight children, I've spent most of my adult life pregnant. Or drunk. After I got sober, I realized the striking parallels between recovery from alcoholism and the process of pregnancy and childbirth. Those similarities inspired this book.

I credit 12-step recovery meetings with transforming my life as much as I do motherhood. In fact, today I could not do one without the other. I've always been a little nerdy and loved to read.

So, when I got sober, the literature of the program really spoke to me. I spent some time considering the three legacies in the 12-step program: recovery, unity and service. These three concepts are like a triangle, recovery serving as the foundation, with unity and service leaning on each other to complete the shape. It's my experience that alcoholism is a three-part disease. In this context, it helps me to think of the word *disease* to mean a lack of ease. Essentially when I feel a lack of ease, I'm anxious, restless, irritable and discontented, until I can find something that gives me that sense of ease. The three parts of the sense are the mind, body and spirit.

Recovery treats the mind. It relieves the mental obsession, which for me was the realization that I was imprisoned by my thoughts of alcohol. Where was I going to get it and how? Did I have good enough plans or hiding places to drink without others noticing? Chasing the buzz alcohol provided became a recurrent, persistent impulse. Eventually it took over my mind and the pursuit of even *the idea* of the feeling of that drink became involuntary despite my attempts to ignore it, control it or suppress it. My mind will tell me even now, after a decade of sobriety that "I'm probably fine, I can probably drink normally again." That's crazy, because I live such a lovely life today...why would I try it? Only an insane person would take that risk.

I'm not in charge of the crazy things that fly into my brain, but I'm totally the boss of my responses. This wasn't always the case. My brain used to think I should drink a bottle of champagne on the way to the gym, then drive to pick my kids up from school with a giant stuffed animal sticking out of my sunroof. Today I know my actions have a ripple effect. I must treat my recovery every day so that I can be an asset and not a liability in my own life. When I first realized that, the major question became how could I support my recovery each day by working the other two sides of the triangle: unity and service.

"Most of us have been unwilling to admit we were real alcoholics. No person likes to think he is bodily and mentally different from his fellows. Therefore it is not surprising that our drinking careers have been characterized by countless vain attempts to prove we could drink like other people. The idea that somehow, someday we will control and enjoy our drinking is the great obsession of every abnormal drinker. The persistence of this illusion is astonishing. Many pursue it into the gates of insanity, or death. We learned that we had to concede to our innermost selves that we were alcoholics. This is the first step in recovery."

(Chapter 3, page 30 in *The Big Book of Alcoholics Anonymous*, "More About Alcoholism.")

Unity treats the body. I believe this means both my physical body and the body of members of the 12-step group. I had to get my body into treatment and dry out. I had to get my ass into a chair regularly at 12-step meetings. I had to *feel* raw and broken and *speak* it out in order to heal. I had to *listen* with my ears to those who had started down this path before me to hear how they did it. My body had to *feel* uncomfortable and get comfortable with being uncomfortable. As a result, I had the privilege of *seeing* with my own eyes how people recovered. I also felt the power of the group's individual and shared experiences. Eventually I developed with my brain a belief that I could too, and now I have a desire with my heart to practice a sober lifestyle.

"Life will take on new meaning. To watch people recover, to see them help others, to watch loneliness vanish, to see a fellowship grow up about you, to have a host of friends--this is an experience you must not miss. We know you will not want to miss it. Frequent contact with newcomers and work with each other is the bright spot of our lives." (Chapter 7, page 89 in *The Big Book of Alcoholics Anonymous,* "Working With Others.")

Service treats the spirit. To me, this means getting out of my own head and assisting someone else, another one of God's kids. It's developing empathy for others. It's becoming a helper and working shoulder to shoulder with others, without judging and thinking I'm better than or worse than someone else. It's becoming a seeker of a Higher Power, a God of my own understanding and letting that Higher Power pry open my hands which I have gripped so tightly around my life, which is simply in an illusion of control. It means letting go in order to gain everything. It means acceptance and knowing that if things were meant to be different, they would be. It means prayer becomes less about talking to God and more about getting quiet so God can talk to me...through meetings, books, nature, readings, conversations or whatever else. It's practicing humility and open-mindedness. It's cultivating a teachable heart and a coachable inner tree.

"Abandon yourself to God as you understand God. Admit your faults to Him and to your fellows. Clear away the wreckage of your past. Give freely of what you find and join us. We shall be with you in the Fellowship of the Spirit, and you will surely meet some of us as you trudge the Road of Happy Destiny. May God bless you and keep you--until then." (Chapter 11, page 64 in *The Big Book of Alcoholics Anonymous,* "A Vision For You.")

Essentially, I realized that these three legacies mirror three trimesters in a couple of ways: first, you have to *get pregnant.* Or get sober. That is the foundation of a pregnancy and childbirth that cannot be escaped. Let's say you want to have a baby. I mean, physically give birth to a baby. Of course, there are other options if you want to build a family—adopt a child, find a surrogate or become a foster parent—but for the purpose of this example, assume "you" want to experience childbirth. First of all, you need to have the correct components: ovaries, sperm and womb. Second, there is a period of gestation. If your fetus doesn't complete the period of gestation, you have a miscarriage or baby with some physical challenges and you're facing possible NICU time. I have had two miscarriages, so I know from painful experience that gestation needs to happen in order for fetal viability. At the time of this writing, doctors say that is about 24 weeks. Without the proper parts and the necessary time, you cannot give birth to a baby.

All three of these concepts are dependent on each other. For those of you who want the brass tacks (my fellow members of the "Keep It Simple, Stupid" Club), I will elaborate.

The first thing you need to do when you want to have a baby is get pregnant. Likewise, if you want to give birth to a whole new life, you cannot continue to live the same way you always have. In my case, that way of living included chugging wine, champagne and vodka to escape my thoughts and feelings. Every day. This is not particularly healthy for anybody, but as the mom of four small kids, responsible for endless carpools, class projects, doses of antibiotics and matching socks, it was insane. So what I'm trying to say is that I needed to get sober.

The next thing that must happen for a viable pregnancy is the regular pattern of growth. You need to take care of yourself, take your vitamins, get regular checkups, listen to your doctor's advice. In my most recent pregnancies, I routinely encountered those adorable fruit comparison lists to illustrate fetal growth. If you have no idea what I'm talking about, I'm jealous. Just kidding. Let me break it down. There are tons of different versions, but basically your baby is the size of a fig at 10 weeks, a lemon at 14 weeks, an eggplant at 22 weeks and so on until you get to the watermelon. To grow in recovery you also need to take care of yourself. Regular meetings, following directions from a sponsor and working through the steps.

The third trimester is when you deliver the baby, the miracle of childbirth.

It's exciting, terrifying and unpredictable. Once that tiny human exits your body, you're stuck with it. No return policy, no cancellations. We're "talking final sale, my friend." Of course, motherhood is the most amazing gift I have ever been given, and I'm ridiculously grateful. I know there are many people who don't have the privilege to experience parenthood. But, the delivery is just the beginning. This is how I personally experienced a new life, had a spiritual awakening as a result of the step work, and continue to watch the promises come true in my life: by carrying the message of hope to those who are still suffering, and attempting to practice these principles in all my affairs.

After one gives birth, there is a feeling of overwhelm. That's the best way I can describe it. Just overwhelming joy, overwhelming pride, overwhelming unknowingness of what to do. Getting sober and giving birth are equally overwhelming. Both feel like your goal is to make one trip from your car to your apartment after grocery shopping. Your wrists nearly breaking off, you load 84 bags of groceries onto your forearms and begin the journey up four flights of stairs. When you reach the top, you're thrilled with yourself. You feel electrified and exhausted but overjoyed. But only after you've endured all that pain.

"We have found much of heaven and we have been rocketed into a fourth dimension of existence of which he had not even dreamed." (Chapter 2, page 25 in *The Big Book of Alcoholics Anonymous*, "There is a Solution.")

Pain is the price of admission. Is it worth it? You bet your belly it is. (Pregnant belly or your beer belly, whichever applies.)

1

CONCEPTION

THE START OF A JOURNEY TO A NEW LIFE.

HAZY, blurry confusion enveloped me like a wool sweater on a sweltering summer night. I felt a jarring impact on the right side of the 6,000-pound suburban mom-mobile, but muscle memory kept me driving, hands gripped tightly to the steering wheel. My pulse raced. My head throbbed. My mouth was dry, my eyes glassy. I remember thinking, 'You're okay, you just need to get home." Trees and bushes whizzed by in a bouquet of various shades of green. From the back seat I heard the small voices of my four kids, though I couldn't make out what they were saying.

"Shut up!" I barked. "I need to concentrate!"

Disoriented, I realized I was stopped at an intersection. A woman in a blue sedan in front of me was looking in her rear-view mirror. She parked, exited her vehicle and began walking toward me. I gulped and thought, "I think I'm supposed to put my window down." I groped around on the armrest clumsily and lowered the window. The driver didn't actually approach me, she simply inspected her bumper quickly, looked at me and waved me on, as if whatever had just happened wasn't worth doing anything about. I exhaled and wondered how long I had been holding my breath.

Proceeding forward, I used every ounce of concentration I could muster. Using their middle fingers, a few other motorists communicated their disapproval of my inebriated driving. Several horns blared as they sped past me, but I tried not to let the distractions break my fixation on arriving home safely. After all, I was a responsible mom who had her kids' best interests at heart, clearly.

Fumbling around, my open hand engaged the coffee cup sitting in the console cup holder on a bed of receipts and gum wrappers. I raised the cup and shook it to gauge its contents. Nothing. I considered trying to reach behind me in an attempt to grab the plastic jug of cheap Popov vodka rolling around on the floorboards beneath my children's tiny feet.

A stream of perspiration paraded down my spine like a string of pearls and pooled into my bra strap. My hands slid across the wheel in their own mess of sweat-challenged epidermis.

Through a foggy head, I began to get my bearings. I was on Gilcrest Avenue, the main artery through town. Minivans and SUVs were inching by me. I could just make out the profiles of shadowed drivers, some violently waving their hands, some holding their phones up.

Why were they staring at me? I wondered. How rude!

"I hate people," I said out loud. In the background of my thoughts, I could hear my kids anxiously talking in raised tones from the back seat, my youngest daughter choking out a muffled cry.

My rearview mirror displayed a Fourth of July-worthy display of red and blue lights flashing. Muddled as it was, my brain told my right foot to depress the brake pedal, which I did, with more force than I intended. Suddenly, I couldn't breathe. I needed air. Shakily, I pressed the button to lower the driver's window. My efforts to piece together what was occurring in real time were met with little success. Just then, a gust of wind rushed at me from the side, blowing my hair back. Discombobulated, it took a few seconds to discover I was staring at the silhouette of a backlit police officer.

EMBRYONIC STAGE

GENERAL GROWTH PATTERN FROM FERTILIZATION TO BIRTH.

LYING on the medical exam table, I watched the shapes and images dance across the black and white sonogram screen. It was baffling to think that the moving object on the monitor was actually inside me, and it was a human being. I was baffled, awestruck. It was my first of many such onscreen meet-and-greets, and I stared at that two-dimensional embryo in absolute wonder. Back then I was convinced I was going to be the best mother of all time, or at least since the first female dinosaur laid her eggs. I absolutely believed it was possible to mold and shape this baby into a little version of what I wanted her to be—as if she were a living, breathing, adorable mountain of dough. I'd be the baker, and she would be my perfectly baked creation.

Wild imagination is a condition I have suffered from all my life. The neighborhood where I grew up was filled with original owners of the homes—essentially the cast of *Cocoon*. I was one of only a couple of kids; the other 98 percent of residents qualified for the "senior slam" at Denny's. These old folks were the kind who refused to purchase Girl Scout cookies from me for the entire duration of elementary school. We're talking all the

Girl Scout membership levels, from Daisy to Brownie and all the way up to Cadette and Senior. I mean, I get it, some of those old folks had walkers and it took a good three minutes for them to rise off the recliner, knees crackling and popping. Waiting patiently on the porch, post-doorbell ring, I would hear them stabilize, grip the handles of whatever walking aid they used and slowly shuffle to the foyer. The front door would creak open to reveal a bright-eyed, energetic little neighbor girl selling cookies. My prospective buyers were instantly annoyed. Those were the days you couldn't pause the TV, and we had interrupted their stories. For fear of getting a slammed door in the face, I would waste no time jumping into our sales pitch. Most of the time, my presentation was met with heads shaking and excuses flying.

"I have diabetes," Mrs. Boone would always say.

Marion rarely even let me finish before she said, "No. Come back another time, after *The Young and the Restless*."

Down the block, there was another set of tract homes where I'd had mediocre success in the past. "Sorry, we're on a diet," said Mary Jo's live-in boyfriend (or routine gentleman caller, your choice).

"What do you want?" barked an ever-popular irritable old soul through the screen door from the living room. I remember being aghast, then launching into my spiel anyway. Post-pitch, the person would respond in a gruff and gravelly voice, "Go away! I don't like cookies!" Noted.

Looking back, I feel sorry for those old folks having to get up and come to the door and listen to me. One of those years, it would have been beneficial to make some notes for the next cookie-selling season or remember these particularly crotchety homes come Halloween so I wouldn't have to face them again. These days, *my* kids can't imagine the concept of selling cookies that way. I mean, parents today don't even consider allowing kids that age to venture next door to borrow a cup of sugar, let alone hit the beat on foot to try to sell anything. What can I say, times were different in the 1980s.

Cabbage Patch Kids were all the rage in early elementary school. The backstory that sold these iconic soft-sculpture dolls was that the Cabbage Patch Kids were dropped off by a stork into a garden, where they grew until cabbage harvest time. Which, I guess was whenever they were shipped to Toys R Us. In the box with each "kid" was a set of adoption papers, with a random name printed on a fictitious birth certificate. I'm not joking when I say random; there were some dolls who came with beyond dodgy names. It was as if the creative team working for Xavier Roberts routinely got together on Friday afternoons and drank a case of tequila to fire up their inspirational doll-naming skills. I imagine there would be that one guy who would bust out a ballpoint pen and a legal pad and the team would start spit-balling, throwing out random, garbled mutterings and encouraging each other:

"Yeah, that's a great one, Bill. We'll call this one Oliver. Middle name Clothesoff."

With each new Cabbage Patch doll added to my collection, I studied the face, the clothing and the name, pondering what kind of personality would fittingly accompany this particular cabbage. One of mine came with the name "Yetta Nia"--for real, people. So, I gave her the personality of an exotic soap opera star, *obviously*. I selected Yetta's wardrobe and channeled my inner ventriloquist, deciding what her voice sounded like and what she would be likely to say.

In an eerie coincidence, back then I had eight Cabbage Patch Dolls and today I am the mom to eight actual humans. So, I guess you could say that I started life the way I live it today. Back then, my eight "kids" were basically living their best life in Mountain View in the heart of Silicon Valley, current home to Facebook and Google. Note: it was not particularly cool to live there back then. It was just your normal run-of-the-mill suburb, the red-headed stepchild of San Francisco living in the shadow of Stanford University in Palo Alto.

As a budding creative, my repertoire went beyond Girl Scout Cookie marketing strategies. I created elaborate plays featuring the Cabbage Patch Kids as the lead actors, incorporating a canine and feline component by adding some lines for a couple of our creepy-looking Koosa dolls (the animal version of Cabbage Patch Kids...yep, stuffed animals with plastic faces who wore clothes. *Nightmares for days*). My early playwriting and production career left no stone unturned; the shows were complete with handwritten programs, costume changes and elaborate scenery and backdrops.

I became artsy and crafty, so in a way it was fitting that I lived in a neighborhood full of senior citizens. But instead of knitting, needlepoint or fluting the perfect pie crust, I dabbled in amateur book production. I was a full-service publisher. I would develop fictional characters, write full storylines and create illustrations. The finished efforts were assembled with Mr. Sketch markers and construction paper, secured with brass brads. So I guess this isn't really my first book.

My little brother came along when I was six years old, and around that time, I realized my world was not all about me. Specifically I began to compare and size up my situation to others' situations. Did I measure up? Was I smart enough? Was I successful enough? Was I liked enough? If the answer was no, I would fantasize ideas and create narratives in my head about how I could change those circumstances.

Weekends were spent dreaming and figuring out the secrets to life, God and basically everything, on the swing-set my dad built me in the backyard. I would wrap my hands around the chains, on the highest links I could reach, then lean back feeling the sunshine pouring over me. I'd hang upside down, letting my red hair freefall down my back. I imagined that I would be a famous movie star or singer someday, since I was born in Los Angeles. This made sense to me because, in my mind, all famous people were from LA. I'm pretty sure I thought I sounded like Madonna. In reality I sounded like Sheck Wes and Biz Markie in a catfight. Did I have the *look* of a famous actor or singer? Nah, it would be far more accurate to say I was like your basic token awkward, angsty character in appearance and deed. You know, the generic kid featured in an after-school special--the wallflower in the corner, the mouth-breather with the bad perm and the head gear. Despite this, I was secretly convinced I was amazing.

I WAS in a particular crowd with four other girls in elementary school: Debbie, Darla, Sarah and Sabrina. The Scarsdale School sandpit had a tall spaceship-shaped piece of playground equipment which definitely did *not* meet the safety standards of today's playground. In honor of the rocket, which we hijacked at every recess, we decided to call our group "The Planets." Thick as thieves, we spent as much time as we could together, scaling this spaceship. We would triumphantly mount the top in victory, burning our hands on the intergalactic metal apparatus we commandeered as our own. We sang the theme song from *The Electric Company*, invented make-believe characters and created personalities. We spent hours weaving long pieces of yarn into cat's cradles and practiced walking the dog with cheap yo-yos from Payless Drugs.

For Darla's birthday one year, the Planets took a memorable trip to her family's cabin in the lovely Pajaro Dunes, with views spanning from Santa Cruz to Monterey. Saturday morning, we piled into Darla's father's ATV and he took us four-wheeling all over the dunes. Dear reader, I'm talking no seat-belts, no helmets, and certainly no cares in the world. We rock-eted at speeds that were probably, in reality, completely cautious and safe, but felt like the *Indiana Jones and the Temple of Doom* ride at Disneyland. We rode standing up, hanging off the roll bar with one arm, flinging the other arm around in the sky as if we were on the steepest plunging dip of a roller coast-er. We did not even consider for a hot minute that we should, at the very least, keep our limbs inside the vehicle. Sand and dirt flew out from beneath the powerful tires, and our small bodies were tossed side to side as the vehicle jolted and rocked. We laughed and screamed as the turbulent wind whipped our hair back, which was a welcome bonus, as this was the era of feath-ered 1980s hairstyles. I remember the adrenaline rush, the feeling of invincibility, like we would live forever, as if we were untouchable. It was the innocent belief that life was ours for the taking, as easily as Scooby-Doo and Shaggy solving a mystery in 30 minutes.

The Planets were in a Girl Scout troop together and my mother was one of the leaders. Our annual Girl Scout camping trip was the highlight of our season, a pilgrimage of fun and good times, where we earned something like 72 badges in one weekend. One year was not so fun, however. I remember setting up camp in this old lean-to type of shelter with the rest of the girls. The Planets, of course, unrolled our sleeping bags next to each other. Except Darla. Darla unrolled her sleeping bag next to Kella, who was not a member of the Planets.

I remember yelling out to Darla, "Hey, Darla! We're over here!" I motioned for her to get her stuff together and make her way over to join us. Apparently, Darla didn't hear me, as she continued unpacking, setting out her pillow and smoothing the pillowcase. She proceeded to ignore me for the entire weekend, without explanation. A couple of times I tried to ask her if I had done something wrong or hurt her feelings. She would turn and start talking to someone else or walk away. I hated the feeling; it was perplexing and sad. I felt left out, confused and alienated. Immediately I assumed whatever was up with Darla had been my fault.

One afternoon during the campout we donned our Zips and set out on a hike. It was a steep trail, but I wasn't paying attention. I was meticulously rolling over the conundrum with Darla in my mind. As I was internally attempting to relive my past encounters with her in an effort to figure out what I might have said or done wrong, my thoughts were interrupted by a loud belly-flop-worthy splash. Some of the adults were standing at the edge of a drop-off hollering, with their hands cupped around their mouths to produce maximum volume. While I was busy obsessing over Darla, one of the troop leaders had fallen off the ledge, plummeting into the river below! Thankfully, she was just fine, although she had been wearing a heavy coat which was now saturated with rotifers, amoeba proteus and other microscopic creatures. I felt as if it were me wearing that soggy coat. The weight of Darla's dismissal plagued me for the remainder of the trip and throughout the school year.

It was the first time I felt rejection and emotional abandonment. Darla was one of those "light-switch friends." She was on, or she was off, either I was in her vortex or I was out of it. Instead of investing in friendships that were more consistent and reliable, it seemed all I wanted was to try and tap dance and shuffle ball change to get something from Darla that she wasn't capable of giving. I figured if I was fun and funny and made jazz hands and spirit fingers when she was "off," she would turn "on" when I inserted myself into her world. This was a game I learned young, and it was a principle I continued all throughout high school. I would find the one person who I was convinced didn't like me and focus my time and energy on winning that person over, instead of gratefully investing in those around me who were already my friends.

As a child, I liked attention. If I wasn't getting it, I'd figure out a way. I remember one such attention-seeking episode on a lovely spring day in 1984, when we were scheduled to do the Mother's Day concert. Our class filed into the school's (very appropriately named, I might add) multi-purpose room when it was our turn to sing a song, called "The Little White Duck" by Burl Ives, to be followed by a rousing all-school rendition of "Free To Be You and Me" by Carole King. We filed onto the stage, the taller kids, of course, ascending the squeaky climb to the top riser. Every single year Brendan Cohen was on the top row in the middle as he was easily the tallest one in the class. I stood next to Aaron Piker, in the front row, stage left, with the rest of the shorties.

I carefully surveyed the crowd. It was a warm day, so there were mothers in sundresses or tennis attire, plus a smattering of grandparents dressed in their plaid golf shorts and Los Altos Country Club polo shirts, methodically fanning themselves with flimsy Xeroxed programs. Dads were generally not in attendance at school events in those days, as it was still considered the father's job to be the main breadwinner outside the home. Thirty-five-millimeter cameras were poised, ready to snap a few pictures with extra flashcubes and rolls of film close at hand, just in case. Those who were into the new technology of the times sported fancy Polaroid cameras on neck straps. There was a roar of happy chatter among the audience members. A few even waved to each other across the crowd.

Our principal, Donna Barry, stepped up to the microphone and cleared her throat. She had the body type of Arnold Schwarzenegger and the voice of Sylvester Stallone.

"Good afternoon," Principal Barry's deep voice boomed through the crackly speakers. Then she performed the universal sign for "shut-the-hell-up," which is to extend one's arms forward and quickly wave them up and down. A hush fell over the crowd, with the exception of one lone whiny baby in the back row, who was clearly not impressed with the quality of the program so far.

Ms. Barry introduced the songs we were about to perform and took her seat in the front row. Nonchalantly, she flipped her Dorothy Hamill haircut and slipped her reading glasses onto the bridge of her nose as she buried herself in the program. Our pianist, Mrs. Bradley, struck the first few chords of "The Little White Duck," and suddenly it happened. I heard it first. It was the most unique, most peculiar sound, almost like a high-pitched air horn, but completely muted. Like what I imagined a small mouse would sound like squealing with delight at the sight of a hunk of cheese. It turned out that cheese was definitely involved, as in, someone had just cut the cheese.

Initially, the smell was faint but it quickly expanded into a rich, thick, matured, fecal odor. I looked to my left at Darcy Dickson, whose eyes met mine in a shared sideways glance. Her lip curled upwards and she turned toward me in an accusatory manner. Trying not to draw much attention, and completely incensed that she would assume that I had been the phantom farter, I simply made the most non-dramatic "ew" face I could muster. Darcy smiled at me, satisfied that I had not violated the air with that smell, and I smiled back with a shrug. As the sulfurous smell continued to swell, I glanced to my right and discovered the perpetrator. What I thought before was a really bad fart smell turned out to be an odor phenomenon beyond all reason and comprehension. The force radiating off the originator of the smell—the epicenter, so to speak—completely enveloped me. It was the strongest, most horrific, wretched, nose-hair-singeing smell my poor senses had ever encountered. My eyes began to water as I looked right at Aaron Piker's face, which was as red as a Roma tomato.

Just then, it was time for us to sing our first line. The rest of the class opened their mouths to sing "There's a little white duck, swimming in the water, a little white duck, doing what he oughter..." but I just stood there, paralyzed by the smell. Aaron was now looking at his feet, shifting his weight from side to side which, of course, only began to move the smell in rapid waves through the atmosphere. Baffled and unable to breathe or do anything else, I suddenly began to giggle, just a little bit at first, but then I felt the laughter gaining momentum. I attempted to stifle the giggles, which was a mistake. Almost against my will, I let out the biggest, loudest snort ever—like the shot heard round the world. Because I was in the first row, the microphone Ms. Barry used was quite near where I stood. Because the microphone remained *on* after the introductions were completed, it was picking up nearby voices and sounds. You could hear several audible gasps from the audience, as the microphone echoed the snort at full volume and the soundwaves ricocheted off the walls of the multi-purpose room.

After that, our performance became your basic shitshow. Try as I might, I couldn't hold my laughter in, and several of my classmates were laughing too. I looked at the audience and could see several adults in front trying not to chuckle. Shoulders were shaking, lips were pressed together to muffle laughter. A couple of people had strategically placed hands over their mouths in an attempt to look as if they were in deep thought over the complex and profound song lyrics. The song continued, as I guess Mrs. Bradley had just made the executive decision that "the show must go on."

Most of my classmates continued to try to sing as best they could through their laughter. "A little green frog, swimming in the water..." To distract myself from the smell that was still affecting my cognitive function, I scanned the crowd. Unfortunately, my eyes locked with Ms. Barry's. She glared at me with a look I'll never forget. Her expression communicated that I was possibly the most lowly, inferior, disappointing student she had ever encountered—doomed to a future of redundant, menial tasks. Her look said I would clearly grow up to be Sisyphus from Greek mythological fame, condemned to spend eternity rolling a giant boulder uphill.

Then I saw my teacher, Ms. Archuleta, and her demeanor wasn't much of an improvement. She looked at me with a cross between utter shock and "I might hang you by your toenails after this and rip your eyebrows out one by one." Slowly, Ms. Archuleta rose from her seat on the bleachers as the laughter continued and made her way to the side of the room where she switched on a large box fan behind Mrs. Bradley's piano. The fan began to whirl, which caused Mrs. Bradley's hairpiece to unexpectedly detach and take flight. It blew right off her head and slid across the floor like a rat with no tail scurrying to the other side of the room. The few students who had maintained their composure became unintentional soloists at one point: "A little black bug, floating on the water..."

Of course, the fan only spread the smell of Aaron's shame throughout the space. As I helplessly continued laughing, I wondered if I dared to sneak a look at Mrs. Bradley. When I did, she was still sitting there in her teal jumpsuit, Candie's and wig cap, diligently banging away on the piano, as if she couldn't smell a thing. She glanced up at me and shook her head slightly as if to confirm that she had never before encountered such an unprofessional musician.

Finally, after what seemed like an eternity, the song ended and the audience managed a weak round of pity-applause. Mrs. Bradley scrambled off her piano stool to retrieve her wig, and students from the other grades began to file into the room for the grand finale of *Free to Be You and Me*. Before I could blink, I felt a fierce tug on my shoulder and found myself being whisked off the platform and ushered straight out the door, along with Aaron Piker. Ms. Archuleta launched into a lecture that blurs in my memory, but by the end of it, I was fairly certain she was going to hog-tie us both. She clearly wanted to throw us in the back of a Los Altos School District utility van, drive us to Fresno, and leave us for dead in a pile of tumbleweeds outside the prison.

This incident occurred several years prior to my mom's campaign for a position on the Los Altos School Board. To my great relief, the fact that her daughter was the "Ruiner of the 1984 Spring Sing" appeared to have no bearing on the outcome, and my mom won the election, so all was well.

Like many other kids that age, I soon learned that it did not feel good to be out of favor with my teacher and principal. I did not like that feeling, not one bit. I became very concerned about staying in the good graces of my parents, church leaders and teachers because receiving praise and positivity from them felt awesome. I realized pretty young that certain behaviors produced positive results, and that was the beginning of my lifelong crusade to try and figure out what would make others happy. Because if I made them happy, I felt good. I've never been a math scholar, but it was a simple equation.

I began to adopt a way of life that I remained committed to for years: impression management. To feel better and to fit in, and to make life more palatable for everyone, I decided it would be better for me to not own my feelings. In my mind, I tried to stuff them away because I didn't know what to do with them, like that old Halloween costume one year when I dressed as a cluster of grapes. I popped the balloons and stuffed it under my bed because I didn't know what to do with it. Problem solved.

So back to the pregnancy websites that love to compare the

size of your growing fetus to a piece of produce. At six weeks, your baby is as big as a pomegranate seed, they say. By 12 weeks, the fetus is the size of a plum. At 20 weeks it is as big as an artichoke, 30 is a honeydew melon and 40 weeks is a pumpkin. Just as my babies grew each week inside my womb, my emotional chaos grew, commencing in childhood.

Growing up in the San Francisco Bay Area provided many opportunities to consume sourdough bread, as evidenced by my thighs. Anyway, there was this sourdough bread-related fad in the 1980s that I'll never forget. This is usually how it went down: someone's mom would toss you a "bread starter" which was a Ziploc bag containing a squishy, beige, unidentified matter as you exited their Volvo after summer day camp.

"Give this to your mother!" the other mom would shout over the roar of the engine. "The directions are taped to the side!" Sure enough, there would be a purple-inked ditto copy affixed to the side of the bag, explaining the process.

Sourdough bread has a very distinctive tangy bite and if you add a bunch of sugar, it becomes Amish Friendship Bread. Who knows if it is actually Amish. Like the sourdough, this bread starter has an active culture, which converts the lactose in milk to lactic acid. The starter then becomes acidic enough to inhibit the growth of dangerous bacteria, which is great because if you give someone friendship bread, generally your goal is not to kill them or give them a case of dysentery. So you were supposed to keep this Ziploc bag of wannabe bread dough on your kitchen counter for 10 days. First, you just knead the bag. Then on day six, you added flour, sugar and milk. Then after more kneading and goodies, finally on day 10, you make three starters to give away, and you bake your loaf.

It sounds gross, but it's the acid produced by the (non-dysentery causing) bacteria in the mixture that gives both the sourdough and the friendship bread its distinctive taste.

Essentially, the sugar in the Amish Friendship Bread covers the sour, tangy taste of the sourdough bread. Similarly in my own life, I was learning to cover my sour parts with sweetness, a path of least resistance. No one wanted to deal with the sour parts, but they would happily take the sweet. I found this to be true in many facets of my life, at church, with most friends and family, and definitely at school. I began to think it actually wasn't okay to have sour parts. I began to believe that I was weird or weak, and the solution was to add more sugar to cover it up—to throw a little glitter on a turd and hope that no one would realize it was a turd—instead of accepting all parts of me. My church upbringing didn't allow for that. If you revealed doubts or darkness, you were out of alignment with God's word. I felt like if I didn't have all the answers to life and the biggest Bible on the block, then perhaps I wasn't going to be the holiest kid in the church. And if I wasn't that, then what was going to happen to me? Seriously.

So, if something wasn't quite good enough, or getting a reaction I didn't like, I learned to ditch that thing behind a curtain and then throw up the jazz hands and spirit fingers.

There was a small bakery in a little strip mall near our house in Mountain View. As a child, I remembered going there with my mom and pressing my nose up against the glass. I was enamored by all the glistening pastries and layered cakes topped with fondant—so perfectly decorated that they almost looked fake. I would place my hand on the case and walk the length of the store, dragging my hand and leaving fingerprints as I traveled. I wanted to soak up every detail as I marveled at the amazing precision of the baker's hand. Small green cupcakes in the shape of frogs with bulging eyes and bright red tongues. Shiny chocolate eclairs with whipped cream bursting out of the sides. Perfectly layered sheets of yellow and choco-late cake slices with ribbons of pink piping draped effortlessly over the top. I admired the outer artistry, the beauty of their maker's creation. As a child I had a budding interest in art history, as my uncle was a curator for a prestigious museum. Walking through the halls of museums with my cousins, I was inspired by raw talent and the people who created these lovely things, including the stories behind them. Not surprisingly, I was so moved by the baker's talented pastry decoration that my first job in high school was in that bakery. I'd met the baker, who I deemed an artist, and I wanted to be his protege. Years later, when I was away at college, a bagel store set up shop in the space formerly inhabited by that bakery. Oddly enough, that bagel store is where I met my husband and also where we got engaged. It's not lost on me how special it is to have the threads of my childhood woven into the coat of my later life. It also explains my paralyzing and oh-so-debilitating addiction to carbs.

Just as my uncle carefully selected the pieces of art that best fit his theme, vision and physical space inside the museum, the baker decorated those breathtaking profiteroles. My focus became ensuring that I presented my finest baked wares. That way, only my gingerly and decadently decorated sweets were in the display case, and the not-so-cute ones were stuffed on trays in the back alongside the everyday loaves of bread.

I got busy deciding what was going to be considered top shelf on my philosophical bakery case, as well, things like positivity, generosity, faith, kindness and loyalty. Then there were the traits I deemed unacceptable for public viewing: my doubts about God, my fears, the difficulties I faced in my relationships with others, which mostly included my perceptions of emotional abandonment and rejection. I learned to decide what was to be shared, and what parts of me were too much, or too lackluster for others to see.

My goal was to always have enough sugar present to cover

up the sour taste in the sourdough. But what I didn't know then was that all ingredients are important, from the most popular and elaborate confectionaries, to the tangy sourdough loaves, to the Girl Scout cookies that my crotchety old neighbors never purchased (those chumps). I mean, may they rest in peace.

I gained 30 pounds the summer I worked at the bakery. In a pregnancy, sure, that's acceptable. Clearly, impression management was taking a toll on me by the time I reached high school and I looked to eating my negative feelings to escape them. All of that emotional chaos had to go somewhere. Just like a growing baby in a belly, eventually it was going to make its way out, one way or another. But in order for that to happen, you must face excruciating pain—that's when the real labor begins. When the black and white images on the ultrasound screen turn into a three-dimensional baby in living, breathing, vivid color.

3

BRAXTON HICKS

PAINLESS, IRREGULAR CONTRACTIONS WHICH
DON'T PROMOTE CERVICAL CHANGES NECESSARY
FOR THE BIRTHING PROCESS. ALSO KNOWN AS
"FALSE LABOR."

"THE BILLY GRAHAM VAN" was the clandestine nickname I gave to the church parking lot shuttle which picked up the evangelicals who were late for church on Sunday mornings. The "born- again" Christian movement of the 1980s and 1990s was in full swing, and my family was in it to win it! We were at church multiple times per week as far back as I can remember. The Jim and Tammy Faye Bakker scandal? Yes, please. I mean, Jesus and waterslides? Consider me there. We weren't "C & E" (Christmas & Easter) Christians, no ma'am. We were card-carrying members. I'm talking baptized by full immersion, you feel me?

My dad taught Sunday school, and at home, he was the handyman type, putting love into all assembly or general maintenance endeavors. He is also responsible for some creative custom inventions. For example, he's probably best known for his handmade one-of-a-kind carpet dash mats, which were uniquely crafted, hand cut for a precise fit to your vehicle's dash board. I mean, who wants a lame old factory dashboard cover when you could have a custom piece of shag carpet?

When he wasn't buried in carpet scraps brandishing an X-Acto knife, he was usually fixing something, peering into a toilet tank with a flashlight or hovering over a car engine, covered in grease. And so, it was often my mom who would drive me to youth group activities. She'd don her large late-'70s sunglasses with the low sides, clean out the carburetor (my dad's classic technique for coaxing our vehicles into performing at optimal levels), and down the driveway we'd float. Moments later we'd be jamming across Foothill Expressway with the safety windows rolled down. Captain and Tennille would be on the radio, or on a really good day, we'd enjoy "Summer Breeze" by Seals & Crofts. My mom would crank up the volume of the crackly speakers and belt out the lyrics at full volume, tapping her fingers on the steering wheel: "Blowin' through the jasmine in my mi-i-ind."

By the time I was in junior high, church had become my home base. School was meh—just okay. I struggled to find a crowd of buddies. The elementary school crowd I'd been palling around with had dispersed a bit, as I was in the choir while the rest of the Planets were all in the symphonic band. They were in honors classes while I was in Math 1A, not exactly the class taken by future Silicon Valley tech execs. It wasn't my old buddies' fault they were studying and taking Mandarin on weekends, while I was practicing dance moves I'd learned from Solid Gold and flipping the channels back and forth between Doogie Howser, M.D. and Saved by the Bell.

My good friend Julie and I spent our non-school hours doing all the junior high youth group things at church. Every Tuesday during the summer, we boarded either the Billy Graham van or the church's converted stick-shift school bus and headed over the mountains to the Santa Cruz Beach Boardwalk, with or without an overheating vehicle incident. For $13 you could ride roller coasters and eat churros all day long. Early autumn brought crisp night air, and at a church junior high all-nighter, our youth staff buried pumpkins in the sand all over Twin Lakes Beach. They set us free and we piled out of either the church bus or the BGV like clowns falling out of a clown car, in the classic combination of adolescent excitement and awkwardness. We took off running toward the beach like the cast of *The Outsiders* in a cloud of jackets and flip flops, and our knees hit the sand as we ferociously started to dig with our hands in search of pumpkins.

I remember that feeling; the rush, the thrilling freedom. Squeals and laughter echoed in the darkness as the moonlight danced off the expansive blanket of the Pacific. I remember the feel of the cold, damp sand between our toes and the gritty texture on our fingers as we dug. It felt like the most important thing in the world, and it was at that moment. We relished in the invigorating and unconventional challenge of triumphantly delivering a smooth, ribbed sphere of squash out of the ground. The prize for the first to do that was a ticket to Great America, the theme park in Santa Clara. My friends, for a Bay Area tween, this was like winning the lottery.

The emotional makeup of my adolescence was interesting. I wrestled with owning my faith for my own self, while juggling my doubts and questions about God. I had the garden variety teenage angst of trying to figure out who I was and where and how I fit in. The narrative I was telling myself was that if I didn't present a grammatically correct, polished version of myself to the world--and especially to the church--I was going to get busted. By *someone*, for *something*. If God himself didn't have time to strike me down with a holy lightning bolt, then maybe he would appoint some finger-wagging old church lady or some rude, misogynistic old man who probably believed women couldn't teach men. I was once busted for applying lip gloss in church, by a lady who said she was "appalled." Another time, an usher wouldn't let me bring a sealed water bottle into the sanctuary. I mean, what if I did something *really* sinful, like watching *Three's Company*? You know, that risqué show involving two females and one *male* living together as room-mates. I mean, wasn't that show produced by Satan himself? Sometimes I felt like I was holding myself together by Scotch Tape because the inappropriate, potty-mouth side of me might ooze out if I wasn't careful. As a result, I felt fairly uncomfort-able in my own skin.

Witnessing for Christ, of course, was a paramount theme of the Evangelical Christian Church. I became convinced that God was going to zap me with His wand of eternal torture if I didn't win souls for Christ. But, like, exactly how many souls are we talking here? And how often? What was the formula to stay in His good graces? I mean, others could possibly go to hell and burn for all eternity, but hey, no pressure. Sometimes I felt like Christianity was a multi-level marketing scheme, like the church was the upline, or the pit boss, and we minions were supposed to bring potential "save-able" friends to its doorstep so we could build the congregation, as well as the pile of cash in the offering plate, provided by the minions' parents, of course.

Some days the minutiae of my life would feel light and easy, carefree and joyful. Other days, I'd feel rejected and worthless. It seemed like everyone else was moving smoothly through their teens, but my growth was awkward and sporadic, resulting in nothing of substance. Just like Braxton Hicks contractions. It wasn't okay to feel pressure, to be out of sync or take extra time to process. It was all about following rules based on what the Bible said. Hmm. It was okay to ask questions, as long as the answer was always "Jesus." From my perspective, I never grasped that my feelings were an ocean, with a rhythm, an ebb and flow, and that was normal. It didn't mean anything was wrong with me. Rather, emotions could be viewed as human experience that I could choose not to act on but instead, just let pass. It would be a long time until I learned that valuable lesson.

Mountain View High School had an uncanny resemblance to San Quentin State Prison, and at times it felt just like that. I could not find my footing with a group of friends. There were these four girls from my youth group who were in my grade and they were tight. Truly, they were thick as thieves. Might as well have had Pink Lady jackets like the girls in *Grease*. They were nice enough to me, but it was clear they were a foursome that wasn't accepting applications for a fifth member.

As misfits often do, I finally found my tribe. A group of fellow weirdos who had also suffered from several failed attempts to enter the "popular crowds" themselves. Once again, when all else failed, I landed with the choir heads. That was really the gang where I fit, as much as I longed to be cool. We were all somewhat nerdy, somewhat weird and major misfits. We were basically the cast of *Revenge of the Nerds*. You know what? Those are the folks with whom I still fit in best, the ones who march to their own drums, have copious insecurities and often an off-color sense of humor.

I never partied, never touched alcohol, never had access to anything like that and was never invited to gatherings where I might have.

I didn't really even know much about alcohol. All I knew was that my parents would bring a screw-top jug of something called Carlo Rossi to our widowed next-door neighbor, Martha, when we'd go over there for the occasional dinner.

"Gerri!" Martha would chide as she teetered around on her Candie's heels under her leathery tanned legs. "Why do you let Randy bring over that cheap Carlo Rossi chablis?" Her earrings would jangle as she moved and laughed, and sometimes she'd forget to put her dental bridge back in after dinner. I gathered that the Carlo Rossi chablis wasn't all that bad.

During my high school years, I mostly just lived with my nose buried in a *Sweet Valley High* book, wondering what it would be like to have a boyfriend and drive a VW Cabriolet convertible. I was a dreamer, and I had some intense feelings. Because of my church background, I thought there was something wrong with me because I wasn't happy all the time. No one told me it was okay to not feel okay. That it was okay, and even normal, to feel out of place.

Still heavily involved in our youth group, Julie and I spent our weekends at high school church events and retreats, playing "chubby bunny" on the bus choir tours, venturing to Mexico to build homes and visiting the shut-ins (elderly church members who were too frail to leave their homes) and laughing later over pizza about which shut-in had the most cluttered garage or the worst smelling house.

Summertime brought church camp, where we made fools of ourselves during team relay races, waterskiing in embarrassing high-cut swimsuits, making up skits and listening to speakers. Driving through every fast-food establishment in the greater South Bay, volunteering at Vacation Bible School and learning how to burn CDs off Julie's dad's computer.

Instead of continuing summer employment and weight gain at the bakery, I decided if I was ever going to land myself a boyfriend, I'd better move on to the Palo Alto Nordstrom, which I did the following summer. Imagine my annoyance when I was assigned to a department called "Town Square" where the average demographic was women age 65 to death. I was relegated to selling wool-gabardine pants (er, are they really called slacks?) St. John blazers, velour housecoats and Easy Spirit shoes. Departure for college couldn't possibly come fast enough.

At some point in my elementary years, our church hosted the Azusa Pacific University Choir while they were on their annual tour through California. I remember watching those lovely, mature, God-seeking girls in their fancy dresses and Robert Caruso steam-curled hair, thinking, "I'm going there. I'm going to be singing for Jesus with a shiny choir uniform and big Sammy Hagar hair." I applied to APU and Biola, deciding Biola was clearly the more Christian of the two, literally because it was called the "Bible Institute of Los Angeles." Obviously, that was the choice for me. APU, on the other hand, was located in a sub-par suburb of LA, across the street from a Sizzler and a Burger King. Thumbs down. Then, at the last minute, I visited my good friend Debbie at APU and felt a vibe—a vibe of fun, of connection, of friendship, authenticity—and that was that. I made a last-minute switch and decided to go to APU. As a dorm-warming gift, I bought myself a Robert Caruso steam hair roller set for the choir days, which paired nicely with Aqua Net Hairspray and a teasing comb.

In college, I got an on-campus job as a...wait for it...Campus Safety Officer. Imagine Paul Blart from *Mall Cop* minus the Segway. Once again, my nerdy side emerged, but I had a great group of friends and did all the wholesome but fun things I could. We ate the leftover food we found in the teachers' lounges, investigated the "Panty Bandit of '97" at Engstrom Hall and snuck around the cadaver lab in the science building, attempting to scare the shit out of each other. Basic tomfoolery. Around this time, I was introduced to what I would call some "mild partying." A couple of times each semester, I hung out with my work buddies and maybe had a Bartles & Jaymes wine cooler or something pretty hardcore like that. Don't mess with me, okay? A church girl on the mean streets of LA, attending a Christian college, drinking her quarterly obligatory

Fuzzy Navel. What can I say, I was about as hardcore as they come.

Thanksgiving break of my senior year of college, I was 21. That year, my mom let me have champagne at dinner. Seated at the table, I remember feeling a physical sensation I had never felt before—definitely stronger than the Bartles & Jaymes Fuzzy Navel. I felt a smooth rise to my head, like someone had wrapped me up into a blanket of soft feathers and laid me down on a puffy cloud. Suddenly, I couldn't care less about— well, much of anything. There was a complete absence of self-criticism, wondering if I fit in, or fearing I might say the wrong thing.

My brain felt sharp, creative and alive—as if I had sudden clarity with no effort. Like the old *Wizard of Oz* movie when there's a switch from black-and-white Kansas to brilliant technicolor as Dorothy begins her journey down the Yellow Brick Road. I felt witty and engaged in the social dynamics around me. Energized. Like I knew who I was, and like I belonged. As if I were one of the band members of Guns N' Roses and we were together again, living it up on the reunion tour.

Looking around the table, I felt so much warmth and love for my family, compassion and grace for them all. I was like Clark Griswold from *Christmas Vacation* when he successfully illuminates the exterior of his house after many tries. I was on top of the world, empowered, self-confident, accepted and connected. It was as if God had yanked on the cord of room-darkening blinds and blazing sunshine poured into a pitch-black room. The whole experience was a watershed moment; I discovered that a drink changed the way I felt physically, mentally and emotionally. And I was big-time vibing with it.

Home on spring break during my senior year of college in 1998, I showed up at church, as usual, on Sunday. I noticed a guy there. A new guy. As with every new single person with a pulse who graced the threshold of First Baptist Los Altos Church, there was quite the buzz about him. "Did you meet the new guy, Andrew? He's from Australia!" asked Susie Pearson breathlessly.

"Did you hear the new guy's accent?" squealed Michelle Moore.

"Did you know Andrew just moved into an apartment in Palo Alto?" asked Jan Chopin.

I made a mental note of a few things:

A) He was at church, so he most likely had some kind of moral code and values. Score.

B) If he was here from Australia, clearly, he didn't mind traveling and was possibly adventurous and outgoing. Another plus.

C) If he was living in Palo Alto, he clearly had a job...and with Bay Area housing costs, it was most likely an actual career. Career equaled motivation and drive, at least in my mind. Always a good thing.

We college and singles group folk generally sat in the same area of the sanctuary during the service. I think the official name of the group was "College and Careers." I always thought it was nice the way they lumped the singles into the college group. It was far less depressing that way, instead of separating the singles and calling us something like "Sassy Singles" AKA "The Group Who Clearly Didn't Receive their Mrs. Degrees in College."

Anyway, I saw this "Andrew" from a distance during the service. I cannot explain it, but I was instantly drawn to him. Odd as it sounds, I felt connected to him, and we had not even met yet.

After the service, I noticed a small crowd of female admirers had gathered around him, chatting and hair-flipping away. I put it out of my mind and headed across the street to the Rancho Shopping Center, the site of my former career at the bakery. I went into the new bagel and coffee shop to work on some journaling and reading I had been putting off (#procrastinator).

I had been sitting in that bagel store barely 15 minutes when the door swung open, and Andrew walked in with two other guys from the group. He made eye contact with me, and to this day, I still remember how he headed straight for me with his hand outstretched. I reached my hand out in response and he shook it. His hand was warm and soft, it felt like home. He introduced himself in his smooth Australian accent and added that he had seen me in church and wanted to meet me after the service, but I'd disappeared. Turns out, he had found me serendipitously, of all places, amongst the bagels. We had a brief conversation, and he left with the other guys. I felt strangely electrified, like I had just met someone significant. I scooped up my stuff and headed home, still kind of weirded out by what I felt.

The next day, I left to go back to LA to finish up my last few weeks of school and graduate. When I returned home a little over a month later, Andrew was still hanging around the church, living his best life as the "Baptist Single Ladies' Most Eligible International Bachelor." After all, he was, apparently, *the most interesting man in the world.*

I thought so anyway. One day, I called him out of the blue, and asked what he thought of maybe going for coffee. I was feeling displaced back in the Bay Area. Southern California had left its mark on me and I was starting to regret moving home. Like Austin Powers, Andrew was apparently an *International Man of Mystery,* having lived in lands abroad and traveled at length. He would probably laugh at my NorCal-SoCal cultural adjustment dilemma, but I needed to make more friends. He sounded willing to take me out to coffee to discuss feeling out of place, so we started up a friendship. He agreed to the coffee date and upped the ante by suggesting breakfast. Big spender compared to Silicon Valley guys in those days! Rolling up in his flashy black Acura, Andrew was greeted by my dad who was rocking his signature look: a paint-stained flannel and saggy jeans, which certainly would have earned him a school demerit for dress code violation at my kids' school today. As per usual, my dad's head was buried under the hood of one of two family station wagons, the unfortunate vehicle of choice for our family. When I've asked why, the answer has always been "because you can haul stuff." I mean, I guess. But I hated and still hate station wagons. If I were to search high and low for one good thing about station wagons, here it is: that third seat in the back—you know, the one that faced opposite the rest of the seats? I'm not gonna lie, that part was actually pretty dope. The choices were unlimited: you could play an eyebrow-raising board game on the down-low. For example, it was possible to discreetly play Dungeons and Dragons while bombing down the freeway to the Esprit outlet in South San Francisco. Or, you and your best friend could "smoke" a bubblegum cigarette out of your parents' line of sight. Or, you could eat an entire can of spray cheese on Wheat Thins all the way to Lake Tahoe while listening to Madonna tapes on a Sony Walkman (so as not to arouse suspicion). Plus, people often (just kidding, never) mistook you for the cast of *The Brady Bunch* or *The Wonder Years* kids. Plus, there were endless opportunities to provide entertainment at stoplights for other drivers. Passengers in the "way back" of the station wagon were living the dream—littering, making faces, flashing...the possibilities were endless, especially if the window was down.

I digress. Andrew picked me up and apparently I talked through the entire drive. I tend to overtalk when I'm nervous and this was a five-alarm display of that fact. On our next date, we met up at the church volleyball game in the park. (On *The Bachelor*, they fly in on a helicopter to the Hollywood Bowl, dine on filet mignon and lobster while being serenaded privately by Elton John. In the Christian singles groups, we played sub-par team sports at the park. Be jealous.) Andrew and I started chatting and we decided to ditch that popsicle stand and go to the movies. He always likes to point out at this part of the story that he bought me the super-sized soda and the extra-large popcorn. True...all true.

The next few dates we talked for hours. About life, about God, about our pasts, about our goals. I remember feeling so instantly, deeply and quickly connected to him, like our hearts were effortlessly weaving together in an intricate yet oddly simple fashion. There was something about him—he could make me laugh, he could be serious, he was intense and he was fun. I felt safe with him, and he gave me his full attention when I was with him, as if our conversation was the most important thing in the world.

One evening we drove up Highway 17 early in our first couple weeks of dating and ended up at Pizza My Heart in downtown Santa Cruz. Munching on cholesterol-laden slices of pepperoni pizza on thin, grease-stained napkins, we walked down through the Ocean Beach neighborhood and onto the cliffs overlooking the ocean. We stood looking out across the dark, enchanting sea that stretched out for miles before us, the perfect metaphor for what was stirring in our hearts, as that was the night we talked about getting married. The expansive universe of possibility and mystery lay before us. Conversation turned to how interesting it was that we had become so close so quickly. We just sort of knew we should compose those unwritten pages of our future together. It felt less like a lovesick, passionate infatuation, and more like intuition, an inexplicable certainty that we shared. It made no sense, yet we had a weird understanding that we were supposed to be together. At the time of this writing, Andrew and I are 22 years married, and those hours on the beach are as vivid in my memory as ever.

Like the embryonic stage of fetal development, my early relationship with Andrew happened quickly, but it was vital to the healthy growth of our future. Weeks later Andrew asked me to marry him, at the very same bagel store where we first met. We were sitting at a table drinking coffee and suddenly the guy who owned the flower shop in the Rancho Shopping Center (who was Danny DeVito's doppelganger, may I add) walked in with a massive bouquet of roses. Distracted by this, my back was turned to Andrew, and when Danny DeVito brought the roses to our table, I swung around in confusion to find Andrew down on one knee. My heart was pounding out of my chest as I listened to him propose, and that was the best "yes" I have ever said.

We jumped in the car and headed to San Francisco for the day to purchase a ring, and it was literally like a dream. I blissfully skipped down Lombard Street with my head in the clouds humming "tra la la." True to awkward form, I had the wedding of my dreams followed by the rude awakening of a reality check. We felt like Cinderella and Prince Charming dancing the night away to ABBA songs at our first-class wedding. The clock struck midnight and we boarded our Qantas pumpkin, seated appropriately deep in the coach section, on our way to Australia for our honeymoon. (Not in the airline business yet, we had exactly zero perks.) We had the pleasure of occupying lucky row 42—adjacent to the toilets. The next 15 hours were spent squished into that Boeing 777-300 as tightly as a joey snuggled up in a mum's pouch. For better or for worse, we spent two (ahem) memorable weeks Down Under, and made it back across the ocean. We've stuck together like marsupials ever since.

In those starry-eyed early days, we dreamily grew together into a tiny, embryonic family unit. We built homes in a couple of small, outrageously expensive Bay Area apartments, and later bought a house in Willow Glen, an area of San Jose. I started teaching 10th-grade English. Andrew was an auditor with an accounting firm. Like baby deer staggering together through a foreign forest, we clumsily navigated the ups and downs of the first year of marriage as a double-income-no-kids couple just livin' on love. And we all know where that leads...

4

CONTRACTIONS

RHYTHMIC TIGHTENING PAINS OF THE UTERUS,
BECOMING INCREASINGLY STRONGER AND CLOSER
TOGETHER TO CREATE CERVICAL CHANGES IN
PREPARATION FOR BIRTH.

SO ALL THAT "LIVIN'" on love" resulted in my first pregnancy, our first-born daughter Ashley. At the time, Silicon Valley had a very high cost of living, so Andrew looked into transferring to his company's Seattle office, which we did. It was there I picked my obstetrician, Dr. Nicholson, the same one who delivered all eight babies. Seattle was a tough place to move to, especially for Californians. It was as difficult to break in there as I had heard, and we definitely experienced the "Seattle Freeze," a term describing the natives. The city was notorious for being passive-aggressive, many of its citizens offering inauthentic pleasantries to your face, but not making room for new friends, new members of the gang. It was difficult to dig below the surface to really get to know people. Thankfully, six months later we had Ashley, and it's amazing how a baby will bridge gaps and open doors to friendship.

We spent Christmas of the year 2000 in Boston, visiting my uncle's family. A few times on that trip my nose was assaulted by certain smells which turned my stomach, and upon our return to California, I realized my cycle was late. I had gone off the pill a couple of months earlier, so I took a test the night we got home. Sure enough, two pink lines popped up immediately. I gasped and ran to grab Andrew, waving the test stick in his face.

He was like, "What is this?" Both of us looked at the test, re-read the directions, and stared at those two pink lines. We just thought the natural next step in life was to get pregnant, and boom! It happened pretty quickly and with minimal effort, which was an awesome blessing. The next morning, after barely sleeping a wink, we went out to breakfast. I remember the two of us sitting there, not knowing what to say. It was as if we were both thinking, *What exactly have we done here?* What I've learned since then is that there is literally never a good, right, perfect time to get pregnant. It happens when it happens. I remember staring into my empty coffee cup longingly, thinking if I put coffee into it, surely I'd make a crack baby. I followed all the rules with my first pregnancy, as most women do.

I felt fantastic pregnant. I wasn't huge and uncomfortable, and I had the best time just setting up the nursery, shopping with my mom, enjoying baby showers and dreaming of the perfect mom I was *obviously* going to be. If I saw a mother in the grocery store wrestling with a screaming toddler over a box of Fudgsicles, I would smile at her but secretly shake my head thinking, Jeez, *I would never let my kid do that, what's wrong with that lady?* Trust me, I have paid for those judgments over and over again. I've realized that motherhood is the great equal-izer of women who thought they were in control. I've been that frazzled mom in the grocery store too many times to count. I think I have PTSD from so many similar episodes. To this day, even though I can go by myself sans children, I just order groceries online.

I was due in August. When we moved to Seattle, there was

a resounding agreement from Seattle natives that "you don't need air conditioning here." Well, I wholeheartedly disagree with that statement. I did then and I do today. No freaking way! I remember calling Andrew while I was lying on the couch, barely wearing anything at all, box fans blowing right on me. He was in his nice air-conditioned office downtown, and I would just cry over the phone telling him how hot I was. I also kept track on a calendar taped to the fridge of how many days I would've used air conditioning if I'd had it. Finally, I wore him down. He was so sick of my complaining that we finally got air conditioning about a month prior to my delivery. Since that time, we've put air conditioning in every single house we've ever purchased here. What can I say? He's a keeper.

So my due date rolled around, and my cervix was cooperating, but there was no action. No contractions. It was like my body missed the memo and I was, once again, slightly out of sync. My doctor offered an induction, which I accepted. We called the hospital two hours prior to our scheduled check in for the induction, and were shocked and dismayed to discover that there was no room for inductions at that moment; all the labor and delivery beds were full. Nothing elective was allowed and we'd have to call back in a few hours. I didn't know it then, but that would be a common occurrence in the births to come, I guess lots of people figure in the long rainy Seattle winters when outdoor activities are limited, they might as well make some babies.

Sure enough we got a call that evening that it was okay to come in. I took a shower, Andrew put my hospital bag in the car and I waddled out of the house thinking, *this is the last time I will ever leave my house just with Andrew alone. From this moment on, my life will be forever changed.* It was the strangest concept ever. We checked into the hospital, and my parents and my brother showed up in the labor and delivery room. Dr.

Nicholson entered, kindly and gently explaining that it was probably going to take a very long time, and they should go home to bed and come back in the morning. By that time, he said, I will have probably made some progress and be closer to time to push. He had broken my water and I was now hooked up to the Pitocin. I immediately felt uncomfortable as my parents and my brother left to go home and get some rest. I silently scolded myself. *You're a wimp! This just friggin' started and you're already in pain? You're going to feel like this all night and it's going to get worse!"*

It did get worse hard and fast. Pitocin is no joke! Andrew was a wonderful labor coach. He helped me breathe through the contractions, and he watched the monitor like a hawk, alerting me when they were coming back down. I clung to his hand. After about an hour and a half, I could not take it, and I asked him to please get the nurse. He looked at me a little shocked and thought I was joking. I said: "No, I'm totally serious. I'm in so much pain and there is a ton of pressure and I can't take it anymore. I need that epidural!"

"Ohhh-kay," he stammered and left to find my nurse. The nurse arrived a few minutes later. With a sympathetic head tilt, she shook her head and gave me a soft-spoken lecture, saying that these things take time. Yes, she would call the anesthesiologist, but there was a line of people who were waiting to get their epidurals before me, and the anesthesiologist was currently in a C-section. Reluctantly, she sat down at the end of the bed, pulled up the sheet, and checked me.

I watched her eyebrows shoot towards the ceiling. "Uh, yes, you can get one now, in fact, I'll be right back." She scurried out of the room and by the time I was suffering through my next contraction she was back with an anesthesiologist.

I got the heavenly epidural, Dr. Nicholson reappeared and Ashley was in my hands within the next hour. Apparently, it's not common for a first labor and delivery to progress so quickly. My parents and brother were called back to the hospital at 4 a.m., and they got to meet little Ashley moments after she was born. It was the sweetest, most wonderfully overwhelming feeling to welcome the first grandbaby into the family.

We did crazy things after she was born. We had a bunch of people visit that first night. We watched a movie and had pizza in the hospital. We had barely slept a wink the night before, and now we were running on 48 hours of catnaps. Andrew was as white as a ghost; he's not one of those who can function well on no sleep. By the time we brought our baby home in her little car seat, we were both so exhausted I couldn't even really embrace that "Now we're a family!" moment as we walked into our house. I staggered straight up to my bathroom like a zombie. Now I know why sleep deprivation is a tool used to extract information from spies, informants and hostages. I got in the shower and cried for 45 minutes. Andrew knocked on the door finally and said it was time to feed her again. I tried to pull myself together to embrace being a mother. I mean, I was smitten with my adorable little Ashley, but this was it. I was in charge. It was all on me.

Having a first baby, I found, is similar to what I imagine an arranged marriage would be like. I had no idea what to do. I felt instant love for her, but upon coming home, it took a while to get used to everything. I had to learn to breastfeed, how to deal with all the postpartum stuff. Plus, she wasn't really sticking to the schedule that we were following in the many parenting books I had read. She was clearly doing her own thing, confident and independent, just like she is today. It took time to realize I was not in control, and *that* was the best place for me to be, watching her, waiting for her to show me who she was over time.

I took the mother-baby class offered by the hospital, recognizing in the group many of the same women from the labor and delivery classes prior to Ashley's birth. Settling into my metal folding chair, I let the diaper bag fall loose from my shoulder while I used my foot to rock the ergonomically-designed car seat back and forth in an attempt to soothe six-week-old Ashley, who had started to fuss. Sweating and exhausted, I heaved an audible sigh as I tried to collect myself after the seemingly impossible task of getting both of us dressed, ready and out of the house for the class.

Our group was led by a woman named Mona. We met in the conference room of an office park which I'm sure the hospital rented. "Secret Lovers" by Atlantic Starr was softly playing on the Muzak tape in the background, which was either very strange or super funny, your choice. Mona had Sally Jesse Raphael glasses and a bad perm. On the first day, she wore a T-shirt with the arms cut off (makeshift muscle shirt) that said Frankie Says "Relax" paired with a broomstick skirt and Birkenstocks with wool socks. She had a wrist full of bangles that jingle-jangled as she moved. She took attendance as if this were a junior high social studies class. Next, Mona pulled her frizzy perm into a knot, securing it with the pencil she used to take attendance, and sauntered around the room.

"Let's see a show of hands. Who here is breastfeeding? Bottle feeding?" Her voice was nasal and annoying, or maybe I just hadn't had enough sleep. Several of us glanced at each other and shifted uncomfortably in our metal folding chairs, which were torture for those of us who still had stitches from delivery. A bunch of hands shot up for breastfeeding. A couple of hands rose sheepishly for bottle feeding. We went around the room sharing our experiences, and I secretly wished Mona had brought a timer to limit time for speaking.

Week Two, Mona had neon pink lipstick on and hoop earrings so big I would have bet money you could have fit a can of Crystal Pepsi through them. She coughed and introduced the discussion topic for the day.

"Today, moms, we have two categories to talk about. First, we'll discuss sleep training. Who here is doing Dr. Sears? Other methods?" I gazed around the room, amused by how this scene would look to an outsider peering into the windows. Some ladies were trying to get their babies to latch, clumsily, as you do when brand new to breastfeeding. Some were sanitizing pacifiers, some were adjusting nipple shields. All looked just as disheveled as I felt.

"How about diapers?" prompted Mona. "Raise your hand if you're using disposables. Now raise your hand if you're doing the environmentally friendly *cloth* diapers!" Thankfully most everyone was in alignment on this one. Only two takers on the cloth. I sat in blissful ignorance of the sheer number of diapers I was going to be changing over the next few years and how much I was going to need the convenience of those disposable diapers.

I loved being pregnant and knew I wanted Ash to have a sibling, so I never went back on the pill. I found myself pregnant again quickly, and was blessed with another easy pregnancy. I was beyond pumped to discover I was having a boy. One of each gender? I felt like I'd won the lottery. Again, I felt great throughout the pregnancy, save for a bad case of sciatica which lasted up through the birth. I was due around Thanksgiving, and about two weeks before my due date I had a doctor's appointment. I was three centimeters dilated that morning. Having not packed a hospital bag or anything, I decided to go spend the rest of the afternoon buying some groceries and getting prepared in case my baby boy came early. I distinctly remember being at the grocery store (this is before online grocery delivery was a thing, people), standing in the freezer section looking at the ice cream. Imagine that, a pregnant woman staring at the ice cream! I suddenly felt *something*. Now that I have eight babies, I can feel when my cervix dilates. I now know what that sensation means, but at the time, I didn't know what it was and I remember thinking, *Okay, what was that?*

I finished shopping and went home. Though I felt nothing else, I called my doctor when I went home and used the bathroom, discovering some other signs of imminent birth, which I won't mention in case anyone is snacking while reading. I felt kind of silly because I had just seen the doctor that very day, but he said for me to just come in anyway, which I did.

So with one hand up the birth canal and his face twisted up, Dr. Nicholson asked, "Are you sure you're not contracting?"

I shrugged and replied, "I don't feel anything."

He shook his head and said, "You're five centimeters dilated. I could send you home but you might have to come back. Is your husband here?"

Thankfully I had called Andrew on the way to my obstetrician's office, and he said he would meet me at the doctor's office on his way home from work, which meant by this time he should be in the lobby. Dr. Nicholson left the room to go talk to him, and I got dressed and came out to find the two of them making a plan.

"So do you guys want to head over there?" asked my doctor.

"Does tonight work for you?" Andrew asked him.

"Works for me," replied Dr. Nicholson. I remember thinking, *It doesn't really work for me!* I didn't have a camera with me (this is, of course, pre-smart phones). All my stuff was still at home, for that matter. We left my car and Andrew took me over to the hospital. I remember thinking, *This is weird, is this really happening tonight? I don't feel anything.* I still felt nothing when we checked in at the hospital, but two hours later I was holding our son Alex.

Andrew was so traumatized by seeing me experience the massive pain of Ashley's birth that he focused on getting me an epidural. Again I almost missed my window to get that, and between you and me, since the entire experience of Alex's birth had been painless so far and I'd felt no contractions, I almost skipped it. But I'm glad I decided that was a bad idea at the last minute, because like Ashley's birth, I had a tear and needed stitches. I was grateful to not have to feel that part. I did feel it after Austin's birth, which is another story.

My friend had brought a camera to the hospital for us, so we do have some pictures, thankfully. I remember being surprised at how much hair my new baby had--a thick mass of dark brown, straight hair—and a cute little Harrison nose, just like Ashley's and Andrew's.

Anyway, I had been the vessel of a second miracle. Quick and easy, Alex had just basically appeared on the scene with little warning. I remember feeling so grounded, so much love, as I stared at our beautiful son, almost like now I was *really* a mom. I had two kids and we were a real family. Of course, we had been a family before with one, and really, even with none. But I just had this really solid feeling of wholeness now that I had a daughter and a son. The miracle of it all was a bit lost on me for a few days as I was so surprised still by his early birth.

Prior to having Austin, our third, I had suffered a miscarriage and I had some pretty raw baggage from that. I was so sad that it became impossible to function under the "slap-on-a-Jesus-smile-and-deal-with-it" guise. I prayed, I tried with my whole heart to seek God's help in understanding why these things happen, and to accept the fact that I would never know. But I was just a train wreck until I conceived again. It felt like

God had become that one supremely annoying kid in the third-grade class who would yank the chair out from under you when you went to sit down. Loose threads began to appear in the delicate, thin sweater of my comfortable little world.

I'd go to church with my two healthy, beautiful babies and sing the words to all those worship songs, praying to a God I felt I didn't know anymore, about subject matter I didn't necessarily find true. All the scripture verses I had memorized around the obligatory table of cookies and punch at the midweek church service just seemed to leave my life feeling void of direction. I felt absent of love from the one person who allegedly would never turn His back on me, God. Suddenly, everything I knew seemed to contradict itself. The Bible stories started to seem strange to me. I no longer believed them just because I was supposed to. I questioned them. I mean, two loaves of bread and a few fish fed 5,000, really? Did that actually happen? I wasn't so sure anymore.

I wondered, who exactly was this entity I had devoted my entire life to? He certainly wasn't who I thought He was back when I was seven, sitting on the shag carpet rug in the Sunday School room at church. Images on the felt board characterized him as the white guy with the chocolate brown beard and the flowing-sleeved toga-like gown, red sash and Teva sandals. He was basically a genie in a bottle, a glorified Santa Claus. I wasn't buying this transaction as much anymore. If it wasn't a basic "ask and you shall receive" formula, why was that verse in the Bible? If I prayed for something and didn't receive it, why not? Hadn't I asked correctly? Usually the party line was to have faith, because it must not have been God's will. If that were true, then what was the point of requesting anything in prayer anyway? It's not like you could change God's mind, right? Questions began to erode my faith and confidence in an all-knowing, all-loving God. I didn't get it. I thought the Bible said we were supposed to seek Him when we were hurting and confused. Wasn't He supposed to answer when His children called upon him? Wasn't He supposed to be a comfort in times of sorrow? But the more I pressed into Him, the louder the silence felt.

Going to church started to feel like a chore. Something that good moms were supposed to do, like a parental responsibility not to be left to chance. As if there was a laundry list of basic requirements each mother should meet. Food and clothing? Check. Love and attention? Check, check. Church? Check. But I didn't know who this God was turning out to be. Didn't it say in Romans that if God was *for* us, who could be against us? What if God changed his mind? Perhaps God would turn on me. What if I committed one sin too many? Essentially, the message I was hearing was that the universe is not a safe place.

When I asked for prayer at church, the well-intentioned pearl clutchers would tell me that I had to have faith during these times when God was quiet. But wait, I thought God was supposed to draw near to us when we drew near to Him. Wasn't He supposed to love and care for us even when our behavior was detestable to Him? It began to feel like I was definitely doing something wrong. I wondered if my presence on the planet, my very existence, the core of my humanity, was displeasing to God. So in response, maybe He had decided to give me the silent treatment. But I couldn't say that at church, so I stood there singing the worship songs, feeling like a fake and a phony. If all God wanted from me was for me to love Him and love my neighbor as myself, why did He seem to care so much about spreading the gospel? If I didn't use the Romans Road to lead my friends to Christ, was I essentially dooming them to eternal damnation in hell, where there would be weeping and gnashing of teeth? That seemed like quite an appalling consequence for not forcing my faith on someone. I never considered that maybe, just maybe, we'd had the wool pulled over our eyes. Maybe you really didn't have to go to a seminary to hear the voice of God. Maybe the contradictions in the Bible were there because the scriptures weren't supposed to be taken literally, despite what we had been told. Maybe Christianity got sucked into the vortex of capitalism and politics, just as so many other movements. *Maybe it was never as complicated as we were told it was.*

Stressed out and overwhelmed, I constantly felt like I needed a break. I felt horrifically guilty that mothering alone wasn't enough to fill my deep loneliness. Driven by emotion, I thought maybe I needed to toughen up. Whatever brought me down emotionally would essentially rule my life. I was a slave to my feelings. I felt shame for being so powerless over my emotions, so I just told myself no. I just had to pull up my Christian big-girl pants, slap on my Jesus smile and deal.

During this time, I had started to build some female friendships. I realized a glass of wine or two at a book club or out with friends really took the edge off. It wasn't like I was fixated on alcohol at all, I just had it occasionally. But I started to truly enjoy those times.

Thankfully, infertility is not one of my crosses to bear. In the blink of an eye, I was pregnant again, and so relieved. My mind had gone to the worst-case scenario—that I'd never have another baby—and I was destined to be a barren woman at age 28. Gratefully this was not the case, and Austin was born the day after Mother's Day, appropriately.

Because Alex's birth had been virtually painless, I remember the decision to induce was fairly unanimous among my doctor, myself and Andrew. I couldn't risk another basically painless birth, with two kids under age 5 at home, lest I be stirring a pot of mac 'n' cheese on the stove and randomly pop out a baby without warning. So a planned induction was right up my alley. Again, I had been dilating like crazy with no labor action, so the next day they began to administer Pitocin. The time came shortly thereafter for me to get the epidural, which I did, and I managed to get the timing right in that sweet spot before the Pitocin contractions really kick in. If you've had Pitocin you know that those contractions are on a whole other level compared to natural ones.

The only problem was, the epidural was weird. It wasn't like the ones I'd had in the past. It seemed to be working only on one side. I don't really know if this is a thing or not, but it was a thing to me, very real and very intense. Back in those days, I thought I had to keep quiet and not speak up, as if I might offend the anesthesiologist if I said the epidural wasn't working quite right. (Nowadays, it's a completely different story. I want to be completely knocked out as far as possible without being intubated for basically all medical procedures, which I make very clear long before anyone approaches me with a needle.)

Anyway, I toughed it out with a quasi-epidural until it was time to push, and then I started pushing and my reflexes took off. I went wild without even realizing it. I was suddenly doing the one-legged horse kick, gritting my teeth with my eyes completely locked shut. I heard the nurse yell, "Amy, watch out, you're kicking Dr. Nicholson in the face!"

Austin's birth was captured on video, including when I pooped right before he slid out. What can I say, that video is now a cult classic. I was assigned the "Bill Gates suite" in the hospital, a massive corner room in the mother-baby unit. I'm quite certain it was because it was the only room available, but it was great.

Going from two to three kids was a bigger deal than I had expected. Obviously, we were outnumbered now. During the week, I really felt the pressure of having only two hands, an infant and two toddlers. I felt like I spent all day putting out fires, based on whichever one was burning higher at that moment.

Meanwhile, my husband was hired on at an airline. He spiraled into a deep workaholic mentality, which seemed necessary to climb the corporate ladder. I was lonely, with just my kids all day. I compared my insides to everyone else's outsides. I didn't realize that I'd had three babies in the time it took others to have one. I was completely isolated and consumed with tending my own garden. But it felt like I was in a race against time to see which was going to grow faster, my babies or my resentments.

Prior to Austin's birth, as part of my miscarriage processing, I decided for sure I wanted to have four kids. So that was my plan. After his birth, however, I had some second thoughts, finding myself feeling like I was drowning just trying to keep everything afloat. Maybe I wasn't equipped to handle another one. Maybe I should just count my blessings and consider it good.

My mind was just getting used to the idea of three kids when it dawned on me that my period was late, and I knew what that meant. The decision had been made for me. Looking back now, of course, I'm so glad it was. I just hoped this last one would be a girl. What an undeserved blessing that would be to have two girls and two boys! How lucky I would be! Quite certain that this would be my last baby, I was thrilled to discover at my 20-week ultrasound that she was a girl.

I remember standing in the lobby of my obstetrician's office and as I was about to be led upstairs to my ultrasound (I happened to have his wife as my ultrasound tech) and telling the office staff, "Okay everybody, *think pink!*" They all gave me a generous courtesy laugh, and up I went, thrilled to receive the news that we were indeed having a girl. This was of course, before the first trimester tests where they can pull DNA from the babies' blood. And this was also before gender reveals, so you kind of just got on the phone and called people to announce the news. Maybe I had even put it on my MySpace page. I wondered if perhaps there was a God after all, and my musings and questions were just complete bullshit. At any rate, who knew. I rejoiced.

I was also thrilled that Ava's due date was in February, a day after Valentine's Day, in fact. As the time drew closer, once again I found myself dilating with no contractions. Now having three quick births under my belt, another elective induction was chosen for Ava's birth. Her birth was quick; I don't even remember pushing once that Pitocin drip started. It was like my body got a whiff of Pitocin and she materialized. I reached between my legs and grabbed her under her armpits and helped pull her up onto my hospital gown as that melodious first cry echoed throughout the labor and delivery room. My fourth sweet baby was in my arms quickly, as if she was eager to meet the world—and it certainly is a better place with her in it.

It's overwhelming and hard to imagine, but I was just swept up in the whole magic of being the mother of four, alone with her newborn. At this point, Andrew no longer stayed overnight with me at the hospital post-birth, but he would come hang out all day with baby Ava and me. To give you a little time capsule, this was 2006, so we watched *Napoleon Dynamite* on the hospital room DVD player. I stayed my full two days in the hospital to recover. Rushing home to three little kids was not how I wanted to spend my first precious days with my final (I thought) newborn little girl. I remember both nights sending her to the nursery so I could get a little rest, and then a couple of hours later, the nurse flipped on the dim lights and rolled in a bassinet with my sweet little Ava, ready to eat. I remember picking her up to nurse and just being deliriously happy, almost as if the experience had been a dream. I felt like Mother Earth, having almost effortlessly birthed these four babies who were all healthy and robust. Almost unbelievable. Call *National Geographic*, I was ready for my cover shot (right after an essential visit from the hair and makeup glam squad, obviously.)

Preparing to go home was like game time, and I could almost hear the Rocky Balboa theme song on an infinite loop in my head. Like walking into a surprise party, I was going to walk straight into sheer chaos, and thus the ultimate quest for maintaining stability would begin.

We pulled into the driveway and gently removed little Ava from the back seat. She was dozing peacefully, wrapped up in her hot pink and leopard blanket, tucked into her ergonomic car seat capsule. We walked through the door and like a vacuum cleaner, life immediately sucked in all around me, as predicted. Instantly I felt overwhelmed, harried and scattered, fighting to keep all the plates spinning.

I began to use my time at social events to escape my feelings. I was plagued with fears of inadequacy, both in my mothering and as a card-carrying Christian woman. The concept of alcohol being served at such gatherings was new to me. When I was growing up, church events did not include booze. Things like alcohol and dancing were deemed sinful, like the draperies adorning the windows of the devil's lair. But going to book clubs and my husband's work events became like birthday cake for me—such a fun treat! I could go to an event and have a glass of wine or two and not think about alcohol again until the next time it was offered somewhere. Essentially it was not a part of my daily life. I deeply craved being known and accepted, and I was becoming entangled by my feelings, unaware of how deep down the rabbit hole I was falling.

The afternoons became my sanctuary; the sweet spot where I could unwind, relax and try to feel like a person again. Now that I was done being pregnant, I could really let loose, I reasoned. I began to have a glass of wine or two alone, while folding laundry and watching trashy TV shows. I started to care less about my big feels and look forward to my naptime wine drinking. I figured that was okay because wine was sophisticated, right? I mean, after all, it wasn't like I was plopping down on the couch with a bottle of whiskey. Jesus drank wine, right? So it was probably all good.

When nap time was over, I began to spend every afternoon in the cul-de-sac with my neighbors, drinking while our kids played. We sat, our gym-toned butts affixed to lawn chairs, while the whirl of Big Wheels echoed in the space between the two-story craftsman-style homes. The wine made me feel like an adult again; it was like the catalyst to a connection with my fellow stay-at-home moms. Those wine afternoons served as an icepick, chipping away at the solitary confinement of mothering.

My husband went to work and was able to accomplish all the *things*--mergers, acquisitions, things like that. With a phone call, he could move an airplane. Mostly, I was in awe of the little things he could do. He could place an armful of files on his office desk and *no one would move them*. In fact, *no one would touch them*. He could book a dentist appointment and never have to worry about childcare. It sounds simple, but to me it was unimaginable, and I was insanely jealous.

As for me, I was just another mother on the chain gang, toiling endlessly in the suburban doldrums. I spent my days doing errands, wiping butts, providing kid-approved entertainment, picking dirty underwear up off the floor, coaxing and pleading with my kids to just take one bite of the dinner I'd made. I usually ended up tossing it into the trash then cleaning up a mountain of cereal someone had dumped on the floor of the pantry. I was in the thick of mothering littles, essentially by myself. I was trudging the path, doing the deal.

I showed up to my husband's work dinners, drank with the other spouses and played the part of the glamorous corporate executive wife. Alcohol wasn't just a social lubricant anymore, it was becoming my VIP ticket to feeling confident, mildly interesting and emotionally secure. I began to feel like being inebriated was the only way to feel good. I didn't really like that, because I was becoming reliant upon the booze, at least from a mental standpoint. But during my own personal happy hours I got to walk around in the late afternoon, my hand wrapped around a stemless glass of cabernet sauvignon and cook, pick up the house, have neighbors stop in. I felt on top of the world, magical, alive. Tomorrow could worry about itself. I mean, wasn't that in the Bible somewhere? So I began to drink every afternoon and into the evening.

I didn't notice it until later, but the level of my depression seemed to sink as my alcohol consumption rose. After a while, my despair enveloped me like the heavy, unrelenting San Francisco Bay fog. Even my friends were noticing I was becoming a ghost of a person, a morose vapor that surrounded a body where a real human used to be. Eventually it was obvious this condition was much bigger than I could handle on my own, and I needed professional help. I admitted that perhaps I had postpartum depression. I had heard from a lady at the gym that acupuncture could help. Walking into this simple office with Chinese décor, I remember telling the acupuncturist, "I just don't understand it. I can't really enjoy my life. I have all these wonderful things in my life but I'm unhappy." I would lie on the cold table, listening to the clock tick, my mouth dry and cotton-y from the previous night's drinking. I mean, I won't lie, the acupuncture felt like hocus-pocus, but then again, so did God at this point. What did I have to lose?

Talk therapy was next. I got a recommendation for a therapist whom I found to be very peculiar in mannerisms, appearance and methodology. The sign on his door read "Dr. Nils Morgenstern, PhD." He wore a long trench coat and an old-school felt hat, as if he had just stepped off the Orient Express or was leaving early for his audition at the local community theatre's upcoming production of *Casablanca* or something. I remember "Nils Morgenstern, PhD" inviting me to *lie on his couch* to talk about my issues. While I realize this is still a normal practice for some psychologists, I wasn't having it. I basically grabbed the figurative mic in response to that offer and said loudly into it, "*Pass.*" No way was I lying on this guy's couch, not for all the tea in my acupuncturists' office. I let him know that I could talk to him just fine from the chair across the room, thank you very much. I was not going to recline on the couch of some weird guy with a mole on his nose and a fedora on his head, talking about myself while he just listened and made me solve my own problems. I mean, what the hell was I paying him for? Wasn't it his job to fix me? Plus, who wears a long trench coat and a fedora indoors? Well I'll tell ya who. A card-carrying flasher, that's who. I was not about to add "victim of indecent exposure" to my rapidly growing list of problems. Of course, I didn't mention how much I drank, as I sipped Bud Light Lime from a reusable commuter's coffee mug at 10:30 am. That was none of his business anyway.

The Shakespearean tragedy of my life was the realization that I actually was living my dream. I had a husband who loved me ridiculously, and four healthy kids. I had enough money to live a comfortable life. I didn't have to work outside the home, which I knew was a gift, although I dealt with feeling odiously insignificant. In the grand scheme of things, what exactly was worth escaping?

And yet...I was still drinking. In the quiet shadows of my

mind, I recognized that a villain had moved in. This uninvited guest, this most unwelcome stranger, was slowly beginning to inhabit every room.

I was facing the naked truth that I couldn't seem to stop drinking when I wanted. Cognitively, it perplexed me. I had been able to drink so sparingly in the old days, and now I was drinking every day. In fact, I thought maybe I was drinking so much that perhaps I had earned myself a fast pass to hell. In truth, I was already there.

DILATION AND EFFACEMENT

THE ENLARGING AND THINNING OF THE CERVIX,
CAUSED BY POWERFUL CONTRACTIONS, DURING
ACTIVE LABOR.

LIKE TRYING to decipher the lyrics of "99 Luftballons" before the internet, I couldn't understand what exactly was happening to my life. I just had to figure out how to get back to a ladylike, pinky-extended, one-glass-of-wine-with-dinner (and maybe half a fancy mixed beverage at a respectable hour) drinking style. I mean, sometimes I could drink like in the old days, sipping politely, imagining one white-gloved hand curled around a Waterford crystal sherry glass, intently focused on the conversation instead of finding the next refill. Other days, just normal life would set me spinning in a frenzy of stress and render me feeling useless. A diaper explosion. A child jamming playdough into his seat-belt buckle would require a trip to the fire department in order to free the fruit of my womb from the seat. Another perpetrator spraying a sibling down with WD-40, and the victim becoming too slippery for me to grasp and carry to the shower. A mystery smell in the playroom that turned out to be an entire wedge of manchego cheese abandoned and fermenting under the couch.

Throw a couple of those incidents together in one day and I was an overheated dog desperate for a drink. Upon returning home, I'd leave my owner standing at the threshold, clueless, as I violently ripped through the front door toward the kitchen, toenails scratching on the wood floorboards as I rounded the corner to my water bowl. Shoving my tongue into the bowl, I would lap it up for what seemed like days, water droplets flying out of the bowl and leaving a watery ring at the base.

Admittedly, those nights were terrifying. I would collapse into bed in a daze. In the morning, I would beat myself up about it, consumed with shame. I would hide under my covers and pull the duvet up over my head, eventually sliding out of bed and descending the stairs doubled over like the Hunchback of Notre Dame, willing myself to slap a smile on my face until I could make it to that bar area in the butler's pantry and hastily pour some hair of the dog with a trembling hand.

School was getting harder to manage, and it was a coin toss as to whether or not it was because I had four kids or raging hangovers. Probably both. Valentine's Day was approaching, and red glitter hearts glued to white lace doilies peppered the walls of the classroom as if a crafting supply store exploded. Stations were set up in little clusters of mini-desks all over the room. One station was for decorating your mailbox, one was for decorating Betty Crocker cupcakes with frosting containing red dye number five. Beyond mess-making and poisoning our offspring with cancerous edible toxins, the goal was to create an epic Pinterest-worthy memory to be posted on social media and admired by all. It was the classroom "Friendship Party," AKA the event formerly known as the Valentine's Day Party. (If you're old like me but don't have kids, you should know we don't celebrate Valentine's Day anymore at school.) I stood in the back, next to a dad I knew who was a police officer for the

Port of Seattle airport as we snapped pictures of our kindergart-
ners on our phones. As I lowered my phone, I noticed the time.
It was 10:38 am. I was already eight minutes late for the first-
grade party, and the third-grade party was going to start at 11
a.m. sharp, regardless if I was ready or not. I hastily scooped up
my preschooler and bolted for the door to make my escape.

"Mom!" I heard my Austin's unmistakable raspy little voice
shout from across the room. Dang. He nailed me. I thought I
could sneak upstairs to the first-grade room for 10 minutes
without his noticing I was gone, but no such luck. With Ava on
my hip, I hurdled over someone's Target backpack hanging off
of a chair. I made my way over to my son and grabbed him by
the chest in a one-armed hug.

"I love you, but I have to run upstairs to your brother's
party really quick," I whispered into his little five-year-old ear,
and I was off.

I flung open the door to Alex's classroom, disregarding the
arc of safety and nearly smacking an office runner in the face.
"Oh shit!" I exclaimed. "I'm so sorry, are you okay?" The
student had automatically ducked and cradled his head in his
arms as if he were doing the "brace for impact" pose on an
airplane careening towards earth. He straightened up and
peered at me over his tortoise-shell glasses in disbelief. I was
unsure if the greater offense was sheer terror because I almost
decapitated him, or the fact that I swore at a Christian school.
Sweaty and overflowing with guilt and disdain, I bolted next
door to Ashley's classroom, snapping photos and helping with
crafts with one hand as I gently clung to Ava with the other. I
was beginning to feel like I was juggling water balloons coated
in oil.

My self-worth was also taking a beating as my role as an
airline executive's wife expanded. The people and the social
culture at the airline were not the problem. Many of these

employees I had known for years. They were inspirationally upbeat, positive and encouraging. They would tell me what a great boss Andrew was, how much he valued his family and how lucky I was to have him. I mean, they were not wrong! Yes, yes, check all the boxes, I was well aware of how wonderful Andrew was. He was on the news, he was giving speeches, he was approached by strangers all the time at the airport who wanted to talk to him. I began to feel as small as a piece of lint on an executive officer's suit.

Don't get me wrong, Andrew was a great dad. He would book me in first class when we traveled as a family, and stay in coach with the kids. Flight attendants would constantly stop by my seat and gush about my amazing husband. If he took the kids to the grocery store, he was praised from the second he entered to the moment the cashier handed him the receipt.

I began to put on those inner "victim" glasses and make everything about me. I mean, no one gave two craps if I took my kids to the store. In fact, I felt invisible, just another one of the typical customers who comprised 95 percent of their clientele —white, stay-at-home breeder moms. If it had been me in coach class with the kids on a flight, not only would no one make a fuss over me, but passengers would probably glare at me. I imagined I could read in their scowls the certainty that my large brood would make it the flight from hell, complete with screaming kids and maybe a food fight.

Sometimes it felt like it was all too much to bear. Every fun activity I tried to plan for my kids, every outing, was met with resistance from at least one of them. I couldn't make everyone happy—ever. I adopted a phrase that I use to this day: "Thank you for submitting your complaint. It has been stamped and filed."

I distinctly remember being in a self-absorbed daze at our local grocery store. (I did actually go to other places although it seems implausible.) The minutiae of my life was suffocating me and an argument that morning with my husband had dampened my spirits. I felt smothered in the reality of my daily world. I did an inventory of my cart, filled with diapers, creamer, kids' snacks and about 14 jumbo bottles of Yellow Tail Chardonnay and wondered if it was enough wine to get me through the week. Then I realized it was already Wednesday. I shook my head and tears welled up in my eyes.

Look at you, I thought to myself as I stared at all that wine. *This is the sum total of your life.*

Waterfalls of tears suddenly spilled over my bottom lids and I couldn't stop them. Petulant, self-pitying, sulky, kicking-the-dirt tears. I felt so small. Why wasn't I fulfilled? Why did I have to drink every afternoon to quell the inadequacies I felt inside? I'd been blessed with four healthy babies. I hadn't had to earn that; it required no skill. I was just freely given these beautiful kids. People much more equipped with patience, love and creativity should have these kids, I thought, not me. I knew there were moms out there who would get down on their hands and knees and build forts with their kids out of pillows and towels. Moms who would line up all the Hot Wheels cars in the backyard and pretend like it was Daytona Beach. Moms who made Jell-O Jigglers into the letters of the alphabet and spelled out their kids' names on a plate. The same moms would dress Barbies up and build a fashion runway out of egg cartons to play New York Fashion Week after naptime.

And then there was me. I felt like a failure and suspected others knew it. Time to crack open another bottle of wine because I couldn't deal with who I wasn't. Just like drunken Ms. Hannigan from the musical *Annie* stumbling over kids at every turn, bottle in hand.

Standing there in the store, a memory of an elementary school piano recital flashed through my brain. I had just been

seated on the bench and the spotlight was on me. I had practiced for this day for months. I had perfected my piece, "Taran-
tella" or the "Spider Dance," and I was ready to shine. I lifted
my right hand to begin and suddenly my mind was blank. I
couldn't remember what note to hit. I glanced at my hand,
which wasn't shaking, it sort of just hovered there, suspended
in midair above the keys. What in the world? Did this ever
happen to David Bowie? Frozen, I just sat there, totally paralyzed, staring at the keys.

Motherhood had reminded me of that feeling of sheer
blankness. I was blowing it, and there were no do-overs. I had
these lovely children and this one small, blessed section of time
to grow and raise them. There was no pause button, no rewind
and replay.

I began to get up on school mornings, still drunk from the
night before, and pour myself a tumbler full of champagne,
hide it in a rarely used kitchen cabinet, and make a full hot
breakfast for my family just so I could pretend that I was a
decent wife and mother. I became a Disneyland mom with no
financial boundaries. I did ridiculous things to overcompensate
for my shitty behavior. Once I bought a giant six-foot stuffed
teddy bear at Costco, put him in the car with his head sticking
out of the sunroof, rolled over to the McDonald's drive-thru
and ordered something like 15 Happy Meals. Still slightly
buzzed from the gym that morning (I don't think I've ever
started a sentence with that phrase before), I almost missed the
turnoff into the school, and had to slam on the brakes and basically power skid into the parking lot. The kids collectively
cracked up at the sight of the ginormous bear rising from my car
like a homecoming queen on a float. I opened the passenger
door, and the smell of McDonald's French fries wafted through
the lot, drawing kids from all over the school, as if I were the
Pied Piper. It sounds like I was the best mom ever, but in truth,

I was overcompensating for my shenanigans. I knew the motive behind those grand gestures. It was a herculean effort to divert attention and counteract any negative suspicions about my behavior. It was all a show, and I had become the Fyre Festival of motherhood.

6

TRANSITION

THE MOST INTENSE PART OF LABOR, WHERE
CONTRACTIONS BECOME CURIOUSLY POWERFUL
AND THE MOTHER DOUBTS SHE CAN COMPLETE THE
BIRTHING PROCESS. ALSO KNOWN AS THE POINT OF
NO RETURN.

LIKE AN OLD SWEATER from the Goodwill, I was officially coming apart at the seams in each area of my life. The more the seams come apart, the more loose ends are exposed, and the yarn starts to unravel. The result is everyone can see what's underneath your clothes and you can't hide anymore.

The consequences of my drinking started increasing. I started having conversations in blackouts at my husband's work functions. I got overly drunk at social gatherings with other moms and it was now obvious I had a problem. This was quite an accomplishment since my neighborhood and its surrounding areas were basically "Lushville, USA." On a few occasions when I carpooled and didn't drive, that's when I'd really let loose. Here's what it looked like to me: I would start out bubbly, fun and confident, then I'd keep drinking. I'd pass the stages of browning out and blacking out, settling into a spaced-out stupor where I'd go quiet—almost comatose. People would take me home and help me get into the house. From the door, I'd stumble to the couch, flip on the TV intending to just "unwind from a whole night of unwinding, and pass out, only to wake up in my clothes. The sunlight would pour in the windows and I'd hear the shower turn on upstairs, signaling that Andrew was awake and getting ready for work. Disgusted with myself, I'd sneak upstairs, rip my clothes off and hop into my side of the bed. As if I really thought he would believe I hadn't been there all night.

By this time, I was your basic hot mess. I drove drunk routinely. I started leaving Post-it notes around the house written in cryptic code so I could remember what I'd said the night before. That way my husband wouldn't have to remind me we'd had that conversation. I'd glance down at the Van Halen symbol affixed to the dishwasher and know that we'd talked about purchasing new appliances. It became a full-time job to keep functioning, and I was well aware that I was doing a shitty job of that too.

Traveling was becoming a challenge. It used to be a fun, memorable break along life's way. Back when I actually cared, I'd typically research fun activities at each destination. But now, I was more likely to look up the liquor laws in each state and make sure I could easily buy booze at a grocery store. When we stopped to get groceries for the little ones, I could pick up alcohol and hide it in my suitcase.

Then there were mini-bars in hotel rooms. Once upon a time, they were harmless, a non-issue, save for one of my kids ransacking it and eating all the chips and M&Ms. But occasionally I found myself doing something I'd never done before. If I couldn't get access to alcohol by other means, I would drink the booze from the mini-bar and refill the little bottles with water. The seal was broken, but if I was careful enough upon opening, you couldn't really tell it had been tampered with. I would always feel a chill wash over me as I carefully replaced the bottles of faux booze on their cold shelf. Sometimes, it was difficult to do perfectly because my hands were shaking so badly. Often, the sober me couldn't really face anything anymore.

Once on a trip home from Beijing, I smuggled vodka in little Nalgene bottles. I knew I'd need it before we'd even get to the airport lounge. We were escorted from our hotel all the way to the plane by a lovely young girl. When we went through security, one of the officers pulled my bag aside and began rifling through it. It was as if she knew where Willy Wonka's Golden Ticket was and she had 10 seconds to find it. Triumphantly she found it and pointed it at the sky like a lightsaber. It was like a slow-motion movie. I wanted to scream "*Nooo!*" but it was too late—she opened it and took a big sniff. Instantly, the officer's eyebrows shot north. She snapped her head to one side, calling out in Mandarin to another officer.

A woman in an official-looking uniform pulled me aside, and I was instantly terrified that I'd end up in a Chinese prison forever. I got out of that one by lying and saying I didn't know you couldn't bring your own alcohol on the plane. I lied to my husband and explained to him those were little bottles of contact lens solution. He doesn't wear contacts, so it seemed plausible to me. Andrew looked perplexed, but was focused on staying the course, so he and the escort began gathering up the bags.

Not surprisingly, my marriage was on shaky ground. My husband was mad at me all the time, it seemed. From his perspective, he couldn't understand why I was drinking so much and why I wouldn't stop. He doesn't drink so it was just a big mystery to him. I would yell at him and tell him he was trying to control me and to get off my back. I just needed a break, and life raising four kids pretty much by myself was tough. He couldn't really argue with that one, so he would forgive whatever antics I was up to and we'd move on.

I had one friend remaining who would still tolerate me. Jen

drank as much as I did, and she let me hide my empty bottles in her recycling bin because her husband drank probably more than both of us combined (which was quite an accomplishment). I took advantage of my free air travel perks as often as possible and Jen and I would take trips and drink ourselves silly. We behaved like teens on spring break instead of the married mothers of multiple children we were. It was pathetic. A couple of times, a furious Andrew came and picked us up from local dive bars after both of our phones had mysteriously died. It was probably more accurate that we couldn't hear the phones ring, since the thud of "Pump Up the Jam" was pounding through the speakers.

Jen and I were wonderful friends but horrible influences on each other. We shared a locker at the gym and we bought cheap champagne and beer at the Rite Aid next door, thinking we deserved a treat while working out. During Body Pump class one day, I remember standing in the back of the class and realizing to my dismay that my weights were sliding off as if the bar had been rolled in butter. It's a mystery to me why we never got kicked out of that place.

As my disease continued to progress, one day I was carrying my two-year-old daughter up the stairs and passed out. I took a nose-dive down the stairs, regaining consciousness only to find my husband carrying me to bed in a fireman's hold. In the morning, he dropped me off at the local ER where an X-ray revealed I had tibia and fibula fractures, requiring orthopedic surgery and the implantation of a rod and four screws.

After the surgery, Andrew set me up in the downstairs bedroom. We both knew that I had fallen down the stairs because I was drunk, but we pretended that was not the case. I was laid up for six weeks, making myself crazy reading mybrokenleg.com message boards, doped up on painkillers, watching reruns of *MTV Cribs* for days on end. Everything became about poor me and my horrible situation. I was a seriously pitiful lump, rocking back and forth in bed, unshowered, in the fetal position, while casted. Your basic Nancy Kerrigan post-Tonya Harding attack, I lamented "*Whyyy* did this happen to *meeee?*" My poor husband, mom and kids patiently helped me as best they could, but I couldn't seem to clear the hurdle of the mental funk I was in. Even I got sick of me.

Not long after I was healed and back on my wobbly feet, I performed my own reenactment of Meg Ryan's classic scene in *When a Man Loves a Woman* by passing out in the shower. I awoke briefly, floating in and out of consciousness as I realized Andrew was blow drying my wet hair and wiping off my bloody face. He put me to bed and when I awoke, I couldn't face the reality of the night before. So I pretended to be unfazed, bounding downstairs in a cloud of energetic positivity.

Andrew was pouring coffee and the smell made me so nauseated I could barely stand it, but I kept up the ruse and said, "Good morning!"

He turned to face me and stared at my nose. He paused for a few seconds, and then replied in a concerned tone, "Morning. Are you okay? Have you looked at your nose?" I shifted my weight as my pounding head felt like someone was lofting a bowling ball onto cement.

I flipped my hair and nonchalantly looked at my nails. I rolled my eyes. "Oh, yeah." I offered, waving my other hand like it was no big deal to collapse in the shower and break my nose. "Totally fine. All good," I reassured.

Later that morning, I dropped into my doctor's office and discovered I had to have my nose reset. Stunned, I asked, "Are you kidding me?" Tears began to fall from my eyes. He looked at me, cleared his throat and shifted his weight.

"Are you sure there's nothing you want to tell me about

how this happened?" I shook my head until I realized my nose was throbbing. He took a breath and continued. "Because if you don't feel safe in your relationship, there are resources available, you know. I can connect you with—"

I interrupted him. "I'm seriously fine!" I said, sliding off the medical nose-chair contraption and wiped the tears with the back of my hands. I hurried out of the exam room and burst through the double doors of the practice. Out in the fresh air, I became overtaken with fear and panic and tried to compose myself as tears threatened to spill. I felt so helpless. If only I could get to the car, where there was a bottle of vodka in the trunk, I would be okay.

One Christmas my husband asked me to go to a program in Orange County where I could work on my issues. He lied and told me it wasn't rehab. He said it would give me a chance to get away from the kids and the pace of life at home to work on myself. To get some intensive counseling and begin work on the long-postponed treatment for the postpartum depression I'd battled since my second son's birth.

By this time, I was in bed all the time. I was drinking around the clock. I could no longer function. I was having to rely on others to take my kids to and from school. My mom had to come up because I couldn't run my household anymore. I had the shakes; I was constantly getting in and out of the shower because I couldn't remember that I had just taken one. I was having panic attacks. My psychiatrist gave me Xanax, so then I was drinking and taking benzos. That was my actual undoing. My husband announced to me that I was getting on that plane, and he personally escorted me to Depression Camp, which I was still telling myself was "not rehab."

Andrew walked me through the front doors of the "not rehab" and I saw a 12-step poster on the wall. Are you—no. No freaking way. "What *is* this place?" I whined. I was instantly pissed that he had lied to me. I cried and begged him not to leave me there. It was pathetic, considering I was a dumpster fire who had just poured gasoline all over her life. I calmed down a bit when I realized at least I got to be somewhere different, away from the shitty mess I'd made of my normal life. Well, I figured, I was going to have to pull out all the stops to convince these folks that I was a normal drinker. It seemed like it was time to pull out the old jazz hands, sparkle fingers and acting skills.

Billy, the intake guy, introduced me to the sober house and my rehab mates. I looked around at that motley crew and felt sorry for them. Those poor assholes couldn't drink! Well, that sucked. Billy escorted me to my room. I wiped my snotty nose on my sleeve—after all, who really cared at this point anyway?

"I'll see you in the morning, sister," said Billy softly as he closed the door. I flopped onto the bed and sobbed. Eventually I realized I was exhausted and I needed to get ready for bed. Accepting I wasn't getting out of this, I unzipped my luggage and unpacked.

Now, Dear Reader, this is the point in this sad tale where I share with you the contents of my luggage. Have any of you out there ever inspected someone's drunken packing job? It's entertaining! I began to pull items from the suitcase, one by one, shaking my head and rolling my eyes. A bikini. I haven't worn a bikini since I was in my 20s. A beanie? I guess in case I planned on robbing a bank. A pair of mismatched high heels. A Seattle Mariner's baseball cap. A hoodie. Some weird-ass striped breakaway-type pants with Velcro that I'd bought as part of a Halloween costume. Some lingerie. An old concert tee with the words "Rush: Roll the Bones." A pair of my husband's jeans that I must have grabbed accidentally. Finally, I exclaimed aloud in pure frustration, "What the hell am I gonna wear for a month?"

I decided to pull a Steve Jobs and pick a basic uniform. If it was good enough for Steve, it could be good enough for me too, I figured. For 30 days, I wore what I affectionately began calling my "Unabomber outfit." The hoodie, the baseball cap, the Rush tee, and the husband's jeans. I added one signature accessory, a pair of massive, clearance-rack sunglasses procured at the local Walgreens we frequented in the big, white 16-passenger Ford Econoline which we called the "Ati-van." The ironic similarity to the Billy Graham van of my youth is not lost on me.

For the next month, I sat there, stoic and full of myself. I paid little attention and refused to consider that I might actually be an alcoholic. I compared my life to everyone else's there, and all I could see was the differences, no similarities. At least, none that I let myself see. I had told myself that I wasn't raised like that. I was too good for it. After all, I'd started out as a normal drinker! And that became my mantra for the remainder of my "not rehab" 28-day vacation. Blinded by pride and ego, I tolerated the weeks and parroted back what it sounded like they wanted to hear. I could not even imagine having all the feelings again.

Okay, I mean let's be honest, while I was drinking, my emotions were all over the place, but it was better than having to face life without liquor. What's more, I was pretty sure I couldn't stay sober anyway. I knew that rehabs required complete abstinence. Jen and I had joked about that before. We addressed the fact that we knew we both drank too much, but we were also clear that going to meetings was out of the question. We thought once you started doing that, you were totally screwed because people would be onto you and watching you like a hawk all the time. We mutually decided that we needed to control the narrative.

One day in "not rehab" we took a walk by an Italian restaurant and I looked through the windows at the large mahogany bar with a granite top. I could see shelves upon shelves of lovely red wine bottles, some in wineskins and some with beautiful art deco and Impressionist-style labels. Desire consumed me. I instantly felt a zing on my tongue. I could taste the flavor and the relief it could bring me. I decided then and there that I would be making my way to a bar as soon as I got to the airport.

Which I did. I faked a nice speech at my coin-out ceremony and I was outta there. I'd show those chumps that I could drink just fine. I was a normal drinker, remember? I told no one I thought I was an alcoholic. My public statement was that I had just gotten a little out of control. Of course, I was secretly afraid that wasn't true and I was worse off than I let myself believe, but I didn't care. I was like Pavlov's dog and the bell had rung. I made my way through security at John Wayne Airport and headed straight for the bar. My heart was pounding and my mouth was totally parched. I slid onto a barstool. The bartender was a young surfer dude in his early 30s. He was tan, with a bleach blond #surfmullet, and game-show-host teeth that looked like mini marshmallows. He smiled and greeted me as he placed a napkin down on the marble bar in front of me.

"Wassup, ma'am!" He said cheerfully. *Ma'am?* I thought. *Fuuuuck.* I drew a breath in sharply and blinked several times, as if I'd just been kicked in the stomach.

"Uh, yeah, hi," I mumbled. I cleared my throat and attempted to sound semi-friendly. "I'll take a glass of cabernet, please, something super dry." He flashed his pearly white mini-marshmallows and nodded.

"Coming right up, ma'am!" As he spoke, his blond surf mullet bounced effortlessly, like a Pert shampoo model's. He turned his back to me while selecting a bottle from the bar.

I sighed deeply and caught myself drumming my fingers on the bar impatiently, wondering why it was taking 845 years for him to choose a cabernet. I drank that wine like a glass of ice water offered to a woman who had just walked through the Mojave Desert in August. I ordered another glass. Then a double vodka and Diet Coke. I drank all the way home on the plane. My husband picked me up at SeaTac, fresh from "not rehab", and I was drunk. He was so disappointed. Well, fuck him. Wouldn't it be nice to be admired and promoted and esteemed at work? I knew nothing of what that felt like. So as far as I was concerned, he could just go fuck himself. I had a suitcase full of resentments with his name written all over it, and I was ready to unpack.

He was baffled by my hostility. He had sweetly created this whole homecoming scene at the house, which I promptly thanked him for as I opened a bottle of wine. The next two weeks were horrible. I just pretty much picked up where I'd left off, minus the benzos, which I had run out by this point. I lied to all my neighborhood friends and told them rehab had taught me how to drink normally again. This was interesting to those who had experience with a family member or knew anyone who'd gone to rehab—but hey, this was 2011, so maybe methods were new? I sold everyone this false bill of goods. I was no longer in denial, but I was certainly not going to let anyone think I was a scumbag like those gross, uneducated derelicts in "not rehab" who had lost their marriages and their homes and had legal problems. I mean, I had standards, people.

7

CROWNING

THE POINT OF LARGEST STRETCHING WHERE BIRTH
IS IMMINENT. KNOWN IN SOME CULTURES AS "THE
RING OF FIRE."

I DIDN'T REALIZE I was mere *days* away from becoming one of those derelicts with legal problems. On April 21, 2011, I woke up early from passing out—before the gas station I frequented was open—and I sat shaking in my car, stomach churning, waiting for 6 a.m. to arrive so I could buy some cheap, lukewarm wine in a box. I remember those semi-sober moments, how tough it was to sit with the quiet, because the quiet held the truth of what I was doing to myself and my family. I felt enraged, sick and horrified with myself. I didn't have a choice but to drink. Quitting wasn't an option. I could not possibly see how I would be able to function without booze. It was the only thing that took the horrible, swirling, dark, debilitating self-seclusion away.

This was mere hours before the nightmare reached its crescendo. I got my boxed wine and launched my day. I drank it all and can't recall exactly what I did that day, but somehow I picked my kids up from school and drove home drunk.

After I was arrested, I vaguely remember my neighbor showing up and loading my kids in her car. Sadly and ironically, she had a son in prison at the time who had killed someone while driving in a blackout. I had another lucid moment at the police station. I remember refusing a breathalyzer test on the wise counsel from some person at a bar once who advised me not to take it. I remember being driven to Harborview Medical Center where another patient, perhaps also under the influence of something, screamed at me, and my heart rate skyrocketed into a full-blown panic attack. They wheeled me into an exam room and did an EKG because I couldn't calm down.

I remember talking to my husband on the phone briefly and screaming, "I am so so sorry! I didn't know I was that sick!" or something like that. I remember him telling me I had to calm down so the medical staff could help me. I do *not* remember them taking my blood to determine my BAL and to this day I'm not sure if they did.

I remember being driven to King County Jail. I remember being strip-searched by a female officer and given my orange scrubs and plastic flip-flops. I was crying and she was shaking her head. I still had a couple of stickers on my body from the EKG and she was asking me what they were. I sobbed and said I didn't know.

Clearly intolerant of people's drunken emotional responses, she said something like, "You don't know? There's *a lot* you don't know!" She started ripping the stickers off as if she were giving an angry bikini wax to an ex-boyfriend.

I remember having a mugshot taken and making a bad joke to the photographer about pretending to be Paris Hilton when she took her famous mugshot. I remember sitting in a holding cell, with these speaker phones on the wall, and calling my house repeatedly.

I remember my dad finally answering the phone and sobbing in desperation, "Dad! I'm so sorry! I didn't know I was that sick!" I don't remember what he said, but I remember how his words made me feel. He showed me a kindness he'd never shown me before, and I certainly didn't deserve it. I remember being given a brown bag with a baloney sandwich and being told by an officer that I'd probably be staying the night. My husband wasn't going to be able to get down there with the bail money before the jail closed. I remember not even fighting that statement. I knew I deserved a night in jail.

I remember riding up the freight elevator with two other people, and thank God, one of the guys glanced at me and quietly mumbled, "Ask for socks." As an officer opened the metal gate of the elevator, I asked and was given that prized pair of socks en route to my cell. My cellmate kindly gave me the basic scoop on what to expect. I remember going out into the common area and feeling a weird camaraderie, like here were the criminals, my peeps, and I clearly belonged with them. I was a criminal now, too. They wanted to know what I had done, and I told them. They laughed with surprise at my story, like they couldn't believe some white bitch from the Eastside had done all that. They seemed extremely entertained.

The longest night of my life commenced. If you've never been to jail, you probably don't know that they leave the fluorescent lights on all night. You're given a scratchy wool blanket for which you're grateful, because it's as cold as a meat locker in there. I was equally grateful for my homie in the elevator who tipped me off to the socks. Tuck that valuable piece of information into the back of your mind, in case you ever find yourself in a spot of trouble.

Jail is not supposed to be comfortable, for obvious reasons. I remember thinking this was it—I could no longer skirt the issue. I was definitely an alcoholic. And I probably didn't have a family anymore. Andrew would divorce me, for sure. My kids would grow up hating me. And mostly, I was unsure if I could actually stay sober.

The cell was drab and cold, which reflected my future. Uncertainty filled the room. Shame enveloped me like quicksand. I began to sober up as the hours passed, clarifying the disgusting truth of my previous days' actions. I had gambled and rolled the dice with drinking for too long and today I had lost.

I remember flopping on my side, looking out the dirty window into the darkness, lit only by the glow of the city skyline. I wondered what everyone under those lights was doing, and if any of them had fucked up their lives as royally as I had? Guilt tightened its grip on my heart, crushing my spirit. I felt a hopelessness I'd never known.

You know how the Westin has trademarked a mattress and bed linen set that they call The Heavenly Bed? Well, ladies and gentlemen, I'm here to tell you that King County Jail trademarked their own signature bed. Their spring 2011 mattress came in a contemporary sage green vinyl finish with smooth lines, topped with the functional feature drunk-tank inmates most appreciate—top-of-the-line rubber. And our cell was *en suite*, with a stainless-steel toilet bowl without a seat conveniently placed right next to our bed. It was the epitome of mid-century modern, a classic balance of retro Alcatraz meets Pelican Bay. Thank you, taxpayers, for your excellent taste and commitment to flawless design.

I memorized every square inch of that jail cell, tossing and turning on that squeaky mattress all night. I reached a point where I couldn't even cry anymore. I felt like the world's biggest fraud. I'd had everything I had ever wanted in life and I had thrown it all away over drinking. I knew that, if I wanted my family back, I was going to have to try to get sober, and despite the intense shame, I felt terrified of not drinking. I was losing my security blanket, my best friend, my coping mechanism. I repeatedly went through the first five stages of grief—denial, anger, bargaining, depression and acceptance—all night on an infinite loop. Finally, I dozed off in a state of exhausted defeat.

In the morning, someone came in and told me I'd be leaving in a couple of hours. Following the directions of my cellmate, I made my bed and we went out to the common area for a gross breakfast. One of the other girls noticed that I wasn't really eating and asked if she could have my food. I gave it to her. Another girl asked if she could have my blanket since I was leaving. I told her yes, but then promptly got in trouble with an officer for giving it to her. When it was time to go, I followed the officer out the doors and back to the elevator, to the holding area, and was given my clothes and belongings. I remember thinking I'd almost rather stay in jail than go home and face my life and the messes waiting for me there.

8

DELIVERY

INFANTS ARE DELIVERED INTO THE WORLD AND LET
OUT THEIR FIRST CRY. THEY HAVE ENTERED THEIR
NEW ENVIRONMENT, EXPERIENCING THE FIRST
MOMENTS OF LIFE OUTSIDE THE UTERUS.

I CHANGED BACK into my clothes and found my cell phone
in my pocket. I forgot that I had talked to my husband briefly at
Harborview. Taking a deep breath, I called him. He answered
and said he was outside circling the block. I was amazed that he
had bailed me out and waited for me. I got in the car and we
commenced the worst car ride ever. He gave me a well-
deserved lecture on how repulsive a human I was. How could I
have done this? He told me he found all kinds of crazy stuff on
my computer that I had looked up. He told me about the bottles
I had hidden everywhere around the house. He told me I was
in deep legal trouble and that Child Protective Services (CPS)
was coming over that afternoon. I just sat there and took it.
What else could I do? There was nothing to say. He was right
on every level, even about some things I didn't know I'd done,
but obviously he wasn't making them up.

Shamefaced, dejected, embarrassed and defeated, I rode
quietly in the passenger seat. Finally, the tears came. They
streamed down my face and dripped off my chin, landing in my
lap. My future felt completely uncertain in every way—with

my family, my finances, my ability to stay sober. I felt totally and completely alone. Helpless and hopeless, like my soul had been ripped out. The backpack of remorse was so heavy I couldn't stand up straight. I got home and my parents were in the kitchen. I couldn't look them in the eye but hung my head in shame. I remember they were so kind to me. They were suffering alongside me in their own way.

My mom suggested I go upstairs and take a shower, which I did. Under the pounding stream of water, I wished somehow it would wash this nightmare away. My head pounded. Everything hurt. Fresh bruises adorned my wrists. Where the fuck did I get—oh, I realized with a twinge that I had been handcuffed and was so drunk I hadn't felt any of the restraining techniques the police used on me until now.

I ran my hands along the glass of the shower door. Coincidentally, this was the same location where I had passed out and broken my nose not long ago. The memory of that event made me shiver, even under 100-degree shower heat. Stepping out of the shower, I was clean physically but felt emotionally filthy. There was nothing to do except go through the motions and face the music. I wanted to run, but instead it was time to face the biggest wound in my aching heart—my four innocent kids whom I had nearly killed.

At the time, my eldest daughter was nine, my sons were eight and six, and my youngest daughter was five. This period of childhood is what I call "the golden years," the ages where they are somewhat independent, but still cute and sweet. They can use the restroom and feed themselves, entertain themselves, but they still think mom and dad hung the moon. I had risked my entire lifelong dream of being a wife and mom, all over alcohol. I had broken my own heart and that of everyone in my family. Though my skin was still warm from the shower, I felt chilled to the bone. The all-encompassing sense of loneliness, alienation and self-hatred was too much to bear.

Trembling, I walked over to the playroom and my knees buckled. I burst into tears and all that came out of my mouth was a noise unrecognizable to my own ears. It was a combination of a guttural sob and wail that seemed to emanate from my very core.

All I managed to choke out was "I'm so sorry, I am so, so sorry!" Kids are resilient in their golden years, which is such a gift. They ran up to embrace me and tell me it was okay. Was it okay? I kept shaking my head as the hot tears poured down my face. It was *not* okay. My children were so sweet, so precious. I knew in my heart I did not deserve their love and forgiveness, and their kind and loving hugs were like a knife to my stomach.

Andrew came in and informed me that Child Protection Services was there and I had to come downstairs. Wonderful. I floated down the stairs, totally unprepared to face any of it.

Miraculously, the CPS guy determined that this was not a pattern of behavior that required CPS monitoring. I was secretly stunned. I thought for sure they were going to take my kids away, but for some reason, he decided that I would be able to care for my kids—and that I had a decent support system in place. He suggested that I go straight back to rehab that very day, and Andrew jumped on the phone to call the treatment center and book my flights. One last note about the CPS guy: he had a very soft voice and his questions didn't feel interrogation. They felt gentle and compassionate, which I deeply appreciated. I won't ever forget him.

I went upstairs and packed for rehab for the second time. Sobbing, packing, sobbing, packing. Weeping, I said goodbye to my kids and my parents. I clung to my kids as if I would never see them again. I cried, they cried. Andrew piled me and my luggage in the car and off we went to the airport. Andrew led me all the way onto the plane. Usually he put me in first class and I would happily drink the flight away, but he had rightfully banished me to coach. I was in a seat that my ego didn't recognize and I had no money to buy drinks. After the guy next to me ordered some double cocktails for himself, I just somehow got the balls to ask him if I could bum some money for a couple of drinks.

He took one look at me, and probably deciding I needed one, he nodded and said, "I got you" in a friendly voice. He bought me two chardonnays. After guzzling them, I felt no change, not even a buzz. All I felt was sadness, remorse, and paralyzing fear of the future. I ignored the side-eye from my kind seatmate, who was probably annoyed with me. This time, I was too broken to care what anyone else thought. Those were my last drinks.

Billy the intake guy was waiting for me curbside in a Honda Pilot, AKA "The Druggy Buggy." I made my way outside from the baggage claim, my head hanging low and my shoulders drooping. I cried when I saw him sitting there, idling in the loading zone. He took me to the detox house and I couldn't sleep, though the accommodations were far superior to those at King County Jail. The next day, all of us fresh off the booze boat, boarded the Ati-van and rode over to the center to see what was popping.

One of the characters I remembered from the center was Dr. Q, a big black lady with a bigger personality. She was waiting for me in the lobby of what I now accepted as legit rehab. As we exited the Ati-van, I could see her silhouette inside, as if she were Norman Bates' mother, just waiting at the window for crazy old Norm's impending arrival. The automatic doors opened and a gust of Santa Ana wind rushed in. Dr. Q shifted her weight, put her hands on her hips, squinted and eyeballed me up and down as my sorry ass slithered into the front office, disheveled, tear-stained and forlorn.

She shook her head, muttering "Mmm-hmm." She grabbed my shoulders and looked me straight in the eye, her piercing dark eyes slicing right through my shroud of shame.

"Are you done yet?" she asked in a tone that said, "News flash: this is a rhetorical question." I melted into her arms. The smell of cocoa butter on her skin was strangely comforting as the tears poured.

This time I finally *surrendered* to rehab and listened. I had to. I became a little bit willing. It was hard. I didn't like it. My counselor was a French shaman named Fred (you can't make these characters up). He looked at me sitting in his office on my first day back. Leaning back in his chair, his elbows propped up on its armrests, he clasped his hands together and rested his fingers on his bearded chin. The silence made me uncomfortable but I didn't have any pleasantries left. I just sat there, sighed and began to pick at my fingernails. We sat in silence for a bit.

Then in his thick French accent, Fred finally asked, "Aimee, what eez problem. Why you no stay so-bear?" I shrugged and said I didn't think I was an alcoholic before all this mess. He nodded and looked off out the window at a large, middle-aged woman walking a massive gang of yipping chihuahuas.

"I cannot feeks for you. You must feeks for yourself," Fred announced. Well, shit. I was afraid of that. My drinking had made a minefield of my life, and here I was twiddling my thumbs expecting some poor soul to clean it all up. Namely, my husband or my parents or this guy. I wasn't really up for fixing my own issues. Why couldn't I just, like, go in for some kind of surgery? You know, have some doctor cut out my alcoholism, get knocked out and wake up with my life magically repaired, like the happy ending of a 1980s sitcom.

I ran my fingers over the bumpy texture of the rust-colored sofa, the piece of furniture I had sat on for many wasted hours during my maiden voyage to "not rehab," a mere two weeks prior. If I had only listened then. If I had only paid attention. If I had only been willing to open my mind to the fact that maybe I truly was an alcoholic. Instead, here I sat, slumped over this ugly couch, facing dire legal problems and a failing marriage.

Despite my protestations, we got to work. I began to follow directions, *even when I didn't understand the directions or the reasons behind them.* I was instructed not to wear makeup. I was instructed to participate in activities that made me super uncomfortable. Fred would routinely find me hiding downstairs, just kind of loitering around the front desk, chit-chatting with the receptionist, Brian.

He'd look at me and say, "Ah! Ai-mee? Why you no go upstairs? You zee, Doc-tear Q is expecting to zee you in Psycho Drama."

I'd sigh and look around and say, "Well Jeez, Fred, ya know, I'm pretty busy helping Brian here organize the paper clips. Plus, my whole *life* is one big psychodrama. I don't need any practice."

Fred, a seasoned therapist who was accustomed to working with addicts and alcoholics, had extensive experience with my brand of snarky, ego-driven comments. He would just shake his head, furrow his brow and point to the stairs. I resisted, but I went. And I listened. I knew that this time, I had no choice.

Over the next four weeks, Fred and I dumped out my junk drawer of denial and baggage, and we began to sort through it, piece by piece, step by step. He taught me the power of rituals, which I had previously lumped in the same category as fortune cookie nonsense and horoscopes, instruments of the devil, thanks to my Christian upbringing. He showed me how empowering it felt to clean up my own messes. Instead of shutting the closet door on all my skeletons, leaving it for the next unsuspecting victim to open, I started to take responsibility.

Fred handed me the basic psychological tools--Maslow's Hierarchy of Needs, the Johari Window, Rational Emotive Therapy—with which to fix my life. Dear Reader, let me just tell you what a surprise it was for me to discover that I wasn't unique. My life hadn't actually been worse than yours or anyone else's, and I didn't deserve your attendance at my pity party. I had to learn to look at the root of my thoughts and perceptions. Let me tell you, this was not easy for me to see at first. It was absolutely mortifying. To be called things like "self-centered" and "full of fear" on a regular basis took some adjustment. Previously I had thought I was a pretty decent contributor to planet Earth and mankind. Had it not been for everyone else basically screwing up my life by failing to meet my endless expectations and demands... Yes, I had to weed all of that nonsense out, and no amount of jazz hands and spirit fingers would get me through this time.

Nope. I felt like a motherless fawn when I left Fred and Dr. Q and the center for the second time. In fact, delivery into my old life was possibly more terrifying than going to rehab. Shaky and unsure, I gripped Andrew's hand on the plane ride home, my eyes locked onto the flight attendant as she walked up and down the aisle carrying mini liquor bottles to passengers. Look, the reality is, that was probably only a couple people drinking cocktails at 10 am. The rest of the beverages were coffee and orange juice, but freshly sober me was always assuming everyone was drinking when I looked through my "booze glasses." I mean, this was a conclusion drawn by a woman who would pour vodka from her purse into her chicken noodle soup at a restaurant while her dining companion was in the restroom. To me, everything was suspect. Accept your invitation to judge me, it only seems fair.

We landed and, as Andrew drove us home, I spouted off about how difficult it was going to be to live in the same neighborhood with the Usual Suspects, which is what I had started calling my neighbors. The same ones who walked me home countless evenings when I couldn't find my house. These were the same Usual Suspects I had lied to just two weeks prior, when I said I'd been cured from *"overdrinking."* Notice how I wouldn't say alcoholism. I imagined their shock and disgust to hear about my DUI two weeks later.

I could just picture them standing around in the cul-de-sac talking about it and laughing, saying, "Well, I hope there was a money-back guarantee on that rehab!" Of course, none of that was true. They were just terribly sad about everything that had transpired and felt helpless. After all, you can't help someone who isn't honest with you.

I walked into the house with trepidation. The kids were napping. My eyes fell immediately onto the area formerly known as our bar. We had a butler's pantry with several racks for barware and glasses. I remembered the care I'd taken to make that area so pretty. We had beautiful martini glasses, elegant long-stemmed wine glasses, old crystal highballs, cocktail shakers, shelving with nightclub lighting and bottles with pouring spouts a la Tom Cruise in *Cocktail*. All the wine bottles were at one time categorized, proudly displaying their colorful labels, resting politely in the chiller fridge. I could close my eyes and replay all the memories in my mind like soap opera flashback scenes with their vignette filters and slow, echoing audio. A house full of friends walking around, wine in hand, chatting, laughing. Me chasing them around, wielding a bottle, a constant refill at the ready. Drinking had been so much fun, an enhancement to conviviality, a balm for frustration, a comfort for sadness or anger. Until it wasn't any of those things anymore.

With a lump in my throat, I ran my shaky fingers across the smooth countertop and just stared at the blank space where that bar used to be. The wine fridge was gone. The pretty wine bottles were painfully absent. I had done a good job of personally making that happen before leaving for rehab. The lovely glasses hanging from their base, the cute collection of wine charms I had collected over the past five years, even the shelving was all gone. All that remained was the delicate condition of my soul.

That evening I saw my kids, who were nothing but gracious, forgiving and perplexingly happy to see me. Of course. But there was an air of discomfort and uncertainty. I felt like a mess of shame, cluelessness and unworthiness.

I realized that weird feeling was eerily similar to one from nine years earlier when we brought my eldest daughter home from the hospital as a newborn. The fanfare was over, the visitors were gone and there were no nurses to help me. We got her home safely, and there I was, feeling exhausted and stupid, and I literally had no clue what to do next. This time, feeling just as tired and lost, instead of bringing home a tiny baby, I was introducing a brand-new me to the family.

It was sort of like "Um, 'kay. Now what?" Since I could think of nothing else, my solution that first night home with Ashley had been to get in the shower and cry for 45 minutes. Sitting there stone-cold sober that night, with my kids asking me about the food at "no-alcohol camp" made me feel like the same solution might still work. Escape to the shower, where I knew I could get away with at least 45 minutes before someone came looking for me.

9

CUTTING THE UMBILICAL CORD

THE OFFICIAL SEPARATION OF THE INFANT FROM
THEIR FORMER SUPPLY OF NUTRIENTS.

MY FAVORITE LINE in the movie *Dirty Dancing* happens at the moment clumsy and awkward "Baby" meets Johnny Castle, the sultry and well-known dance king at Kellerman's Resort. Instead of saying something congenial or articulate, Baby blurts out, "I carried a watermelon."

Well, that was me, particularly in my first few months at home from rehab. Honestly? It's still me, only I just don't care as much anymore, which is liberating. It was time to embrace the awkwardness. There was no escaping it, and for the next few months, uncomfortable feelings were on heavy rotation.

I had all kinds of fun and colorful things to learn. I had to build a relationship with a lawyer, figure out the status of my driver's license and get my vehicle out of the impound lot. Then I had to find a shady car stereo facility (complete with the sketchy clientele, which now included me, apparently) to get an alcohol interlock installed. Weekly check-ins with my probation officer, attending Victims' Panels and, of course, the embarrassing task of telling my neighbors (AKA the Usual Suspects) that I wasn't drinking anymore because I was an alcoholic, as opposed to a harmless *overdrinker*—which I'm sure came as a great shock to them. Eyeroll.

When you become a derelict in the eyes of the state, you don't have to go to jail on certain conditions, including attendance at 12-step meetings. I honestly was pretty *meh* about the idea of attending meetings at first. I am a big fan of having an exit strategy and those 12-step cats were pretty sneaky. They set up around the perimeters so that you couldn't really sneak out the back door easily. Not without getting jumped by several members who wanted to welcome you and pull you into the group. How dare they?

So I planned on getting about halfway into the 12-step swimming pool. I'd do a bit more than get my toes wet, but I had no intention of diving all the way in with those chain-smoking ragamuffins. I had done that with my church growing up, and that whole "all in" mentality ended up biting me in the ass with Jesus. So I was pretty skeptical. Plus, I wanted to reserve my drinking card in case the shit hit the fan and the whole sobriety gig didn't work out. You know, I like to have a couple of plan B's in my back pocket, just in case.

The potpourri of 12-step weirdos who met in church basements and old ramshackle buildings was basically the most interesting mix of folks I'd ever encountered. I was pretty convinced that I was gracing them with my "I still have a house and a husband" presence. Yeah, well, it turns out that Miss Priss was leveled pretty quickly. Like the first time somebody saw my drunk mobile, paint scraped off the rear quarter panel, bent license plate, muffler partially dislodged and dragging. My "Blow and Go" always seemed to select an untimely moment to commence its blaring telltale siren which basically screamed "Attention, attention! The drunk mom has arrived!" It was like walking through the doors of a department store and having the security alarms sound. Immediately I'd scramble to snatch the alcohol interlock unit off its cradle. Dying of embarrassment, I'd shrink down in my seat to blow into it, satisfying its unrelenting demand before any of my new buddies saw me.

I didn't feel like doing any of this, but I didn't have much choice if I wanted my family back. Fred had also instilled a little thought in my head that perhaps it was worth getting sober for myself. What I found odd was that nothing I said shocked anyone in the 12-step rooms. In addition to the nuts and bolts of my new sober life, I was still having painfully intense cravings for alcohol. I wished so much that there was something I could do to take the edge off, something that would help me feel just a tiny bit relaxed. I requested a little meditation area in the backyard, which my dad very kindly built for me, and I would sneak out there and hide for 30 minutes now and then. But as far as a fast-acting magic bullet that required nothing of me? No dice. There was no quick fix, just uncomfortable feelings that were like varying degrees of internal itchiness. Like sitting around in a sandy, wet swimsuit on a too-long bus ride post-beach day.

I began to get invited out to coffee, pie, bowling nights, picnics and all sorts of seemingly lame and depressing sober events. To me, it sounded more like an activities calendar at a retirement community for active seniors. Such events, I deduced at first, were beneath me. Had they all forgotten I was the wife of an executive. Spoiler alert: nobody cared and I shouldn't have either, but that took a while to learn. I came around when I realized I couldn't hang out with the Usual Suspects anymore for fear of drinking again. The list of those who were tolerating me at the moment was short. Thus, I consented to go to a bonfire meeting at someone's house one memorable night and I made some high-level observations.

There was Donald, the recycled hippie in his bell-bottom jeans, wicked John Hughes mullet and Birkenstocks. There was Lola, with the blue hair and the nose ring, who couldn't have been a day over 18. There was Jack, in biker clothes and a do-rag, who always had a toothpick between his lips. There was Margaret with the Irish accent who looked like she was probably President of the Knitting Circle in her long wool skirt, pearls and a prim, tight bun like a cinnamon roll atop her head. As the motley crowd ambled up the street and filed into the hosts' driveway, it suddenly dawned on me how much we resembled the Village People. I began giggling and then busted up into a full belly laugh, which I hadn't done in months. It felt healing.

Minding our business in 2012, Andrew and I discovered I was pregnant with Annalise. This was a massive surprise, as I was a birth control connoisseur by that point in my life. I was still busily attending meetings and staying on top of my to-do list of legal tasks. We announced the surprise to the older four kiddos by handing them a treasure box full of puzzle pieces. When assembled, it revealed an ultrasound photo and a message about a baby joining the family. We had previously told them that we were done having babies, so it was a big shock to everyone. There was screaming, tears and some baffled looks. I had the same reactions a couple of months prior when I got the news from the all-too-familiar set of double pink lines.

Early in the pregnancy, I experienced some bleeding, and our good pal Dr. Nicholson showed us on the ultrasound that there was some blood around the embryo. Suddenly I was terrified that I might miscarry. I had to wait a week to see if she grew, and what a week it was! I knew God would ultimately have her live if she was meant to, and despite my emotions, I knew I had to surrender. Ultimately, she had grown by the next week, and I was overjoyed and elated. Thankfully, I was able to exhale when the doctor told me that as long as she was growing, she was considered a viable pregnancy.

At 39 weeks, the agreeable Dr. Nicholson concluded it would be okay to induce me again, since I had a favorable and collaborative cervix. As if it were a recurring nightmare, the hospital didn't have any beds available on the morning we were scheduled. And so, we waited. My parents came up, we went to breakfast, we drove around and we waited. For some reason, it felt very long to me, and I wasn't as patient as usual. I was tired of waiting and eager to meet her. Finally, around 2 PM, they allowed me to come in and it was worth the wait. In a stroke of providence, luck or magic, I was assigned to the same luxurious birthing suite where I gave birth to Ashley. Annalise was another fast and easy labor. She just slid right into our family, and into our hearts.

Seeing my older kids come meet her was an unforgettable moment. All four of them cried, overtaken by emotion and totally unaware of how powerfully the birth of a sibling would affect them. I was beyond thrilled to have a new baby in our tribe. It felt right, it felt solid, it felt like God's gift to me for getting sober. Annalise was and is the gift I never saw coming. The other lovely thing about bringing Annalise home from the hospital was that it was March, so the older kids were in school all day. Andrew and I had the privilege of just hanging out together with her all day and bonding while he was on paternity leave. We took walks, watched movies and lounged around in bed feeding her and getting to know her with no distractions. It was a precious time and one that stands out in our minds as unique. When we had Ashley, we had private time together, but we were new parents, just learning how to take care of a baby and madly sleep-deprived. This time we were pros. We knew how to care for a newborn and we knew what a fleeting gift that time would be. We were able to focus on just the three of us, so that bit of stress was removed and the entire time was just blissful, delirious wonder.

At the time of Annalise's birth, I was still an active member of the Washington state judicial system. At the two-year mark of my DUI court ruling, I received a personalized, non-optional invitation to the courthouse. Just as I opened the envelope and gasped, baby Annalise promptly filled her pants, which I deemed an empathetic and appropriate response.

Attending meetings and hauling Annalise over to my sponsor's house for step work had become a part of my life. Much to my surprise, I was actually enjoying it. Cleaning up my past, making restitution and turning over my character defects were resulting in small buds of self-love, with the promise of an eventual bloom. But the knowledge that I had State of Washington *case numbers* attached to my name was a most unfortunate and unwelcome thought. On my court date, I left Annalise with my nanny and drove to the courthouse, reframing several times to remind myself how lucky I was to be given a second chance. And that the second chance was actually working. I stood before the judge that spring morning and she commended me for staying sober. I'm not sure how often she sees this whole "get sober instead of go to jail" concept actually work. Smiling, she released me to finish my five-year "sober sentence" without having meeting attendance cards signed. It felt almost like I was kind of...trusted, and it felt wonderful.

After Annalise was born, knowing the close-knit bond that my older four kids had, I made an almost immediate decision to have a sixth baby. I was pregnant with Archer not long after that decision. Interestingly, I went into labor a couple of days before my scheduled induction date. At the time, there was a lot going on at work for Andrew, so it was less than ideal timing. He'd had to miss an important work call with Wall Street, but Archer was born, and I think if asked, Andrew would say that it was completely worth the distraction. Wink.

I was really coming into my own as a 12-step member. Men

and women from all walks of life were there for me. I had a tight circle of women friends who threw me baby showers and brought me meals when the babies were born. They literally showed me how to live sober as a wife and a mother. They showed me how to love unconditionally and how to pick up the phone and get out of my own head when I was stressed out and overwhelmed, feeling inadequate or overlooked. I had been so used to slapping on a Christian smile and quoting a Bible verse instead of just being real and saying, "This shit is hard, and I don't want to admit that, because I know that you'll just judge me and tell me to have faith."

Choosing to get pregnant with Anders, who is baby number seven, was an easy thought process. We just figured we were back to doing diapers, breastfeeding and warming bottles again. Might as well keep going. Boom. Thankfully, getting pregnant has never been a problem for me. It happened so quickly I might as well have been at a drive-thru window ordering fast food. I was pretty sure the girl-boy-boy-girl pattern had been broken when I became pregnant with Anders, because I craved lemonade like a citrus junkie, which I'd craved with all three girls. At 12 weeks pregnant, I received a call from Dr. Nicholson. He informed me that if it really was a girl, then she had a penis. I remember standing in my closet, putting laundry away as my doctor told me that and I burst out laughing. Dr. Nicholson has always been able to crack me up, especially when things start getting heavy or looking bleak. It's a good quality to find in an obstetrician.

I was induced again with Anders, of course. I had a birth photographer, which was a fabulous experience, making me wish I'd thought to do that with my prior deliveries. First of all, we didn't have to worry about trying to get a bunch of pictures while we were otherwise occupied.

Second of all, she was wonderful to work with, took videos

and still photos and was very understanding of the body image issues that came with being pregnant and freshly postpartum with my seventh child.

The anesthesiologist came in and gave me an epidural, which was welcomed. However, my blood pressure shot up immediately and I felt like I was going to pass. Seeing weird spots and lights, I imagined it was what it would feel like to be on LSD or some kind of strange designer drug that causes hallucinations. I tried to remain calm and I just kept telling Andrew that I was okay. I had no idea if that was true or not, but I had this amazing nurse who kept calling the anesthesiologist back in and telling him that she was concerned about my blood pressure and that things weren't right.

Finally, the anesthesiologist just redid the epidural entirely, but I still felt the burning and stretching that they call the "ring of fire," which was always irritating to me during birthing. I was very vocal about not needing to feel the contractions in order to push. In fact, I really didn't need to push anyway. I popped them out like a toaster and I'd gone through an episode of real pushing only once, with my Ashley. Ring of fire or not, my irritation quickly switched to joy as sweet Anders was in my arms in the blink of an eye. His skin was covered in white, pasty vernix and his little scrunched-up face wailed softly into my chest. The sweet miracle of my newborn babies was just never lost on me.

All the while I continued to make my recovery a priority. I brought my sleep-deprived self and my tiny infants to meetings, standing in the back, breastfeeding under a blanket. I made it my policy to leave babies over three months at home with a babysitter. It was always on my radar to try my best to ensure that I was still spending time with the older ones, the "original gangsters," as I call them. We still took lots of trips together, leaving the little ones behind with a babysitter or nanny.

Unfortunately, I miscarried a baby after a European trip with the older kids and had to have two D&C procedures to remove all the tissue. This time, however, I had tools to deal with the sadness of my miscarriage. I no longer questioned God as I had the last time. I was in more of a place of acceptance. Miscarriage is extremely difficult—one of the hardest and saddest experiences that women commonly face—but rarely share with others. Instead of numbing myself, I let myself grieve that pregnancy and that baby who never was to join us in this lifetime. I used the rituals Fred had taught me to heal from this devastating experience. Miscarriage is so interesting emotionally, because even though I already had children, there was something so joyful about knowing that there was another baby coming. Something that felt very promising, very optimistic, in the cycle of life and the chain of the legacy we were leaving. And then to find out that particular baby in my belly was never to join our family in flesh and blood...It sounds selfish because I already had so many children, but a little bit of me died with that baby.

Not long after I had healed from that miscarriage, we discovered Audrina was on her way. I knew she would be my last baby, the very last time I would carry a child, and the thought of that was bittersweet. That pregnancy was tough. Pregnancy over 40 is a whole different animal and it was about time for me to pack up the geriatric pregnancy career. Gone were the days of leaping through the fields gracefully like a gazelle with child, surrounded by wild bunnies and wearing a crown of daisies on my head. Nope. I had reached the point where slowly, over time, I had basically become a pregnant senior citizen, complete with the purchase of adult diapers in preparation for the postpartum leaks. My bladder had become cheesecloth and my joints were aching. Conditions I was blissfully ignorant of in my 20s when I was basically doing Jazzercise on the way to the delivery room and walking out of the hospital in my pre-pregnancy jeans. Finding out Audrina was a girl was shocking and wonderful, and it was straight bananas thinking we had two sets of littles, continuing the alternating-gender pattern, with similar gaps between their ages. At the time, my regret during Audrina's pregnancy was simply that I couldn't show up physically for Ashley's competitive cheer competitions and some of the other older kids' activities. But reflecting as a whole, I think I did pretty well. I showed up for quite a lot, thanks to a new perspective on life where I had told myself it was okay to ask for help, do the best I could and forgive myself of the rest.

I was induced for the last time. We have some great photos of the original gangsters who came down and hung out. Ashley and Ava played glam squad and did my hair and makeup, which had become very on-brand for my births. Alex and Austin helped us with tech issues and went on ice runs. Before rolling onto the bed to become a beached whale ready to receive my usual whiff of eau de Pitocin, I peered down over my belly. My toes were barely visible under the Audrina-bump. Tears welled up in my eyes. I grabbed my phone and snapped a picture of that view, knowing it was the last time I would see myself from that perspective, staring down at a basketball belly. I got my IV, watched the first drop of Pitocin and wheels up. Audrina made her entrance. Dr. Nicholson and Andrew delivered her together, just as with Ashley's birth and every birth thereafter. I exploded in tears of melancholy celebration—that familiar bittersweet fusion—joy courtesy of the regularly scheduled overwhelming hormonal rush of fantastic birthing fireworks and sadness with a side of disbelief at the close of this sacred chapter of child-bearing.

A couple of years later, Andrew and I found ourselves standing on stage behind the podium at the gala fundraiser for the hospital's new childbirth center. As we squinted into the lights, I couldn't believe I was a sober mom of eight, standing up to give a speech in front of all those doctors and donors. Previously terrified of public speaking, I'd developed an ease with addressing groups, one of the many gifts of the 12-step recovery process. As it turned out, that gala was the hospital's highest-grossing fundraiser ever. I'm not attributing it to Andrew and me, but I guess we didn't screw it up too royally, which for Andrew was a given, but for me could have gone either way. Somehow we managed to avoid messing it up, and though it sounds simple, given my past, it's actually quite extraordinary.

10

AFTERBIRTH

THE WOMB BEGINS A PROCESS OF SELF-CLEANING, EXPELLING MATERIALS NO LONGER BENEFITTING THE INFANT. ADDITIONALLY, THE INFANT MUST LEARN THE ONGOING PROCESS OF SEEKING AND INGESTING NUTRIENTS SO THEY CAN GROW.

AFTERBIRTH AND THE POSTPARTUM PERIOD, also called the "fourth trimester," are just...messy. You don't sleep much, your body is a mess, hormones are crazy and your emotions have to catch up with the fact your baby now lives on the outside of your womb. That's just the mother. The baby is learning to find nourishment, communicate and move freely for the first time, even though all they seem to do is eat, cry and poop. Not to mention, newborns are growing and developing at an almost alarming rate. My rehab days and early sobriety were like the fourth trimester. I was learning to feed my recovery, process my feelings appropriately and find my limits. It was busy, hectic, wonderful and scary. Through all the messes, my husband stayed with me.

Despite my fears, I didn't have to move out and get a starter cat to sit on my lap while I watched *Bridget Jones's Diary* in a housecoat eating leftover Stouffer's lasagna out of its oven-safe container. Wait, let's be real here. I do all those things anyway, with the exception of moving out and the starter cat, but you know what? There have been plenty of times I have let life get to me and I have lost my crap and have been tempted to fling open the front door and let out the loudest primal scream "F*ck this shit!" you've ever heard. At least in some circles, I think moving out would probably have been considered the lesser of two evils.

My decision-making while drinking was horrible at worst and questionable at best. But the decision to find all-new playgrounds and playmates has been one of my best. Some of my standards are basically non-negotiable. For me, the big one is germs. Yeah, that's right, I'm a hand sanitizer freak and I was one before it was cool. To the untrained eye, outsiders may think I sound fairly laid-back and casual. Until someone pukes and out come the HazMat suits and the bleach. In my house? If you're sick, you're quarantined in your bed—period. Don't expect to be lying around on the couch with your dirty-ass Kleenex box, moaning for sympathy and coughing your phlegm on healthy family members. Nope. I'll give you a water bottle, send you to your room, bring you some chicken soup, maybe an old copy of Viktor Frankl's *Man's Search for Meaning* and then I'll toss you a bell. Ring it if you need something. Other than that? Consider yourself E.T. zipped up inside the makeshift medical facility. Quarantined—way before it was fashionable.

A couple of years ago was one of those times I needed help, and much to my dismay, I became E.T. in the surgical tent, a scientific-medical spectacle. I didn't want to be there and I certainly wanted to control the narrative, afraid that others might think I had secretly been drinking and had done damage to my heart. I had no choice but to let all that go and just fall into the arms of the God of my own understanding. I didn't cause it, I couldn't control it, I couldn't change it. I couldn't escape it. I was at the mercy of my own health and my body's response to medical treatment. Boom, out of nowhere, I was basically just face down in a proverbial plate of nachos, caught in an emotional tornado.

It all started when I caught a cold on a trip to Spain with Andrew and my older four. I felt sick but pushed through and started having breathing issues and major swelling as the week went on. I thought maybe I had pneumonia or something and just needed some antibiotics. I found out it was far more serious. So when I returned home from Spain, I was sent for a chest X-ray and the doctor chased me into the parking lot as I tried to leave the imaging lab.

"Come back here, ma'am!" yelled the doctor as I looked over my shoulder to see this guy running at me like an Olympic sprinter. Now, I'm originally from LA, remember? I also trained for (and passed) all my tests to join the LAPD, post-Campus Safety days, but I went home and married Andrew instead. What I'm saying is that I have street smarts. So when someone is chasing me, my first inclination is to run. As if on autopilot, my adrenaline kicked in and I tried to take off on my swollen feet but tightness seized my chest and I began wheezing. "Ma'am, *stop!*" commanded the doctor. I had no choice but to do as he said.

"Don't run, ma'am!" he called again sternly. Then he pleaded, "Please come back inside. I need to talk to you."

I felt too shitty to care that he kept calling me ma'am. I slowly turned, shoulders slumped, still gasping for air and began to make my way back inside. Dr. Olympian led me into a room that had the word "Consultation" on the door. At that point, I knew the jig was up. This wasn't good, and whatever the sickness was that I'd been running from for the past week in Spain had now officially caught up with me. The doctor pointed to a chair.

"Please sit down," he said with an element of pleading in his voice. I guess it was obvious I was somewhat of a flight risk mentally, even though physically it was challenging for me to even take a breath.

"Did you drive here yourself?" he asked. I nodded, slumping down in the chair, panting and trying to find a posture that would be comfortable enough to hear what this cat was trying to say. "Well...your lungs are filled with fluid and your heart is very enlarged. Have you ever had heart problems before at all?" I shifted around in the chair, uncomfortably gasping for breath and I shook my head. He took a deep breath and I was jealous because that was something I'd been trying to do for days.

"Okay. Well, I don't know exactly what's wrong with you, but I imagine you aren't feeling very well. I'm going to ask you to please go directly to the ER—do you think you can drive across the street?" I nodded, but honestly, between you and me, I wasn't really sure about that. He handed me a copy of the chest X-ray and said, "Okay, I'm calling over there and telling them to expect you. *Go straight there, please?*"

I nodded weakly because I didn't have enough strength to laugh, but I wished I could. I thought the guy must be telepathic. Not only did I have a lunch date I was entirely intending to keep, but normal Amy would definitely *at very least* go home first, grab some supplies, probably take a shower, place a few phone calls, pack a phone charger, go over the after-school activity plan and put on some lip gloss. I made my way to the ER and called the friends I'd planned to meet for lunch. Now, as freaked out as I was, it wasn't exactly my mission to have visitors see me in this pathetic state, but before I could argue, one of them said, "We're on our way." By this time, I was staggering into the ER like one of the zombies in Michael Jackson's "Thriller" video and I didn't have the where-withal to protest.

Within 20 minutes, two girlfriends, one guy friend, my

Andrew and I were all crowded into a tiny ER patient room. I'm not sure who looked worse—me, all pale and disheveled, or them. Three hours went by and I got a CT scan, ultrasound and EKG. I lay there shirtless under a small towel exposing my saggy, golf-ball-in-a-tube-sock boobs, which saw better days before breastfeeding eight babies. I sort of wanted to care, but I was just too weak. The silver lining was that there was ample space for the nurses to affix electrodes to my chest.

Eventually, the ER doc came in and announced I was at 20 percent of my normal heart function due to a virus that he suspected. For whatever reason, it ended up affecting my heart. I received a creepy "Welcome" bag from the hospital, which is that plastic sack for personal belongings that might as well say "you're not going anywhere." I remained a guest at the Heartbreak Hotel, my pet name for the cardiac wing of the hospital I made my home for the next four days and three crazy nights, the same hospital where I gave birth to all of my babies. My friends who showed up in the ER never left my side—literally. They took turns staying overnight with me and let Andrew go home and be dad so our kids wouldn't worry or think anything too serious was going on. It was astounding, moving, touching. People just kept coming, as if I were handing out some gift. There was nothing in it for them *at all*, except to encounter a gross, sweaty version of Amy without makeup at about 50 percent of my normal spunk and energy level.

My diagnosis was *dilated cardiomyopathy*. For you non-medical types like me, from my understanding, it's a decrease in blood flow due to the left ventricle of the heart becoming enlarged and weakened. To add to the problem, I had a leaky valve. This cornucopia of problems was caused by a condition called *myocarditis*, which is an inflammation of the heart wall that is usually caused by one of several common viruses. Of course, I assumed it was my fault I had this myocarditis. I worried that maybe it was because I drank so much in past years. But I had exercised all my life, didn't smoke and in the grand scheme of things, hadn't been a drinker for very much of my life.

A couple of months later, I still wasn't well enough to avoid having an internal cardiac defibrillator implanted in my chest. A wave of vanity and massive disappointment swept over me. I remember sitting in my cardiologist's office holding a pamphlet covered with photos of mostly male senior citizens.

I turned to Andrew, unfolding the glossy pamphlet and said, "Check this out, babe, I'm going to have the same equipment as my homies." We both laughed and I realized that, similar to joining the 12-step community, I was now in yet another group of old dudes. At least the old 12-step guys were happy, joyous and free. Every time I walked into the cardiologists' office it was like walking onto the set of *Grumpy Old Men*. Nevertheless, it was kind of fun to see what everyone was wearing: lots of socks with sandals, those high-waisted plaid golf pants and Members Only jackets. A year after my heart ICD was implanted, another echocardiogram revealed that my heart function had improved. I was overjoyed and asked when I could have the ICD removed.

My cardiologist smirked, shook his head and answered, "We don't practice that. We just go in and change the batteries. You'll probably have one forever, just like you'll probably be on heart meds for the rest of your life."

This was not the answer I'd expected. I thought to myself, "What in the actual Sam Hill?"

If I was getting better and my heart function was improving, why couldn't I just get this bulky thing removed? It wasn't exactly comfortable, and it was a bad reminder of the incident. Kind of like the scars on my leg remind me of my drunken broken-leg days of 2009. Now my cardiologist was telling me that these annoyances—the ugly, somewhat uncomfortable defibrillator and the heart medications—will be what keep me going strong. Interesting. So the mechanisms that I think are irritating and gross are *actually* the power source to keep me going? Not so different from the 12-step meetings I'd once been indifferent to but now delight in attending. I devour the literature and carry the message by sponsoring others and taking them through the 12 steps. What can I say, I've leaned into and actually love the pieces that help me maintain the joyful life I lead today.

The heart stuff was tough. The alcoholic stuff was tough. It's never fun to be on life's operating table, being sliced open, lying in the recovery room, accepting help to accomplish basic functioning.

Moreover, I know with every cell in my body that my journey had to unfold as it did. Each part of my steep, treacherous walk has been necessary to bring me to where I am today, mostly fulfilled, generally just accepting of myself and in pursuit of a cyclical manner of living and learning, as opposed to a linear one that ends in the non-existent illusion of "perfection." I no longer feel the need to define myself by my perceived failures or successes. I know that I have nothing to prove to anyone and that what other people think of me is none of my business. This is freedom. And like a cool glass of chardonnay when I was drinking, I just want more.

Currently, I am at the end of my pregnancy and birthing chapter. Having babies is not a lifetime career; it's generally a small portion of a woman's life in the grand scheme of things. It's almost weird to type this, since I was "so done" having kids after my fourth, then my entire perspective changed after my fifth arrived. So now, as I approach the end of the childbearing season of my life, I've delivered my last baby. I've nursed her for the final time. I've watched her little newborn body change into a full-fledged baby and then a toddler.

The next season will roll around, and when it does, it will be time to cooperate with God and make that shift. Much like a baby taking her first steps, I might find it awkward and uncomfortable at first. As with any ailment, life-alerting change or season of life, I know I will learn how to maneuver through it when the time comes. A handful of years ago, when my then-two-year-old daughter broke her leg, she was pretty much confined at first to the stroller. Soon, she was scooting around on her bum, dragging that heavy cast around. Not long after that, she was bouncing around on the heel of that cast like a professional. Humans are meant to be very resilient. I don't have to like it, but I do have to accept it. Acceptance of that diversion is where the learning and the gratitude come from, and the result of those efforts is usually where I find my joy.

It's like being in a flight simulator. An inexperienced pilot like me has to assess the conditions, adjust accordingly and leave the rest up to God.

Otherwise, pretty soon, a firm voice urgently booms from the cockpit instructing, "Pull up! Pull up!" I had to make that mental shift when I realized those handcuffs weren't just pretty, silver, knockoff Tiffany bracelets chained together. Or when I saw two lines on a pregnancy test after we were done having kids and discovered a fifth baby was on the way. Or when I found out I was in heart failure and not just in need of antibiotics.

I've learned that the clay of my Higher Power is not glazed, fired and permanently set like it once was. It is not some beautifully decorated cake, sitting behind glass. It's not to be placed on a shelf like a trophy or some piece of art in a museum, just waiting to collect dust. My relationship with the God of my understanding today is like the wet slip of a starter clay: pliable, fluid and dynamic. In college I took ceramics (squeaked by with a D+, thank you very much) and I learned that when you want to start again, or something isn't feeling right, you just add some water, fire up the potter's wheel and start over. Seeing what that piece wants to be, watching it take form and shape between my hands, is a fine metaphor for life.

That's where I am with God. I know He loves me. I know He's with me. I see Him in my children's faces, in a sunset, in the ocean's waves. I hear Him in my kids' laughter, in kind words, in a song and in 12-step meetings. I hear Him when I'm drifting off to sleep and hear my teens and their friends downstairs giggling while making pancakes and bacon at 11:30 PM. The God of my understanding performs miracles. Remember Jen? Well, my good friend who was my drinking buddy got sober about six months before me. We no longer share a beer-fridge gym locker; we let that go a long time ago. What we do share, however, is the experience of a complete transformation of our lives. From drunken moms to deeply connected soul sisters, we have shared so much. I can tell you—sober friends are so much better than the pseudo-besties I met on barstools at karaoke nights.

I no longer need a specific building to recognize the presence of a powerful God in my life; I no longer need Bible Studies and prayer groups and a list of dos and don'ts to follow. I'm not called to witness for Christ in the literal sense. God doesn't give a flying rat's ass how I vote, what kind of music I listen to or if I swear. He doesn't need my praise. He's fine without it—He's not going to melt away because I'm not meeting His needs. All I have to do is connect with Him and be willing to let my will line up with His. Seems doable.

Suffering is messy. Getting sober is messy. Cardiac issues are messy. Having a baby is messy. The deconstruction and reconstruction of faith is messy. Relationships get messy. Messy processes are the unifying tent under which we can all find commonality. Life gets messy, we get it cleaned up and we eventually find dealing with the mess bit by bit is ultimately so much easier than half-assing it and stuffing it under the bed like I used to do. Back at the bakery in the Rancho Shopping Center, I remember watching the baker sift flour, separating the fine from the chunkier particles. I remember thinking he was God-like to be able to control the quality of the dough. We go through these siftings in life, and sometimes we are divinely given opportunities to remove the chunks—the undesirable, unwanted parts. When each sifting process is complete, we can take away what is beneficial and discard the rest. Ultimately, we can see that what remains had actually been there all along.

In the spring of 2020, I heard God the night I celebrated nine years of sobriety. The entire family was on quarantine lockdown at home during the COVID-19 pandemic. It was one of those magical nights that don't come around very often, like Halley's Comet of 1986, or some other genuinely rare occurrence. We looked like a flipping Hallmark movie at Christmastime and I *loved* it. We made dinner together, smiling and laughing at inside jokes. Afterward, my husband and our four teenagers sat around the fire. They individually went around in the circle and told me how proud that I've been living as a sober mom and wife for all this time.

I couldn't believe they were celebrating *me. As if!* No effing way. It is *me* who should have celebrated them. *They* are the ones who have proven over and over to possess unprecedented resilience and the ability to forgive. They've been more than an inspiration. More than a goalpost for my sobriety, they have been the very heartbeat of new life. These are the same kids who were taken home by different friends whom they barely knew when I got too drunk at parties or gatherings to care for them. These are the kids who would be at Costco or a church event and take a big swig out of one of my water bottles expecting water, only to gag on a mouthful of vodka. These are the same kids I drove drunk, not just the one time I got that DUI, but routinely. The DUI is just when I got caught. The same kids whose pictures were on the cover of that D-ring binder containing the police report that my lawyer brought to every meeting and every courthouse appearance. Looking at it gave me chills. This same husband and kids flew down every single weekend to Orange County to visit me at rehab. *Both* times. These are the same kids who would send me letters and drawings to cheer me on and encourage me in those early days of sobriety when I was so uncomfortable in my own skin.

My eldest daughter was the last to speak that evening. When I looked at her, I thought there was no way we could have come this far, pretty much grown up together. It's like someone put me in a time machine, and here I am—fast forward 19 years. Like someone started a movie on child-raising and we skipped ahead to the last scene. So this first, beautiful baby I carried and birthed was the last kid to speak that night. By this time, my *Terms of Endearment* emotions were moving along, but she put me over the top.

She said, "Mom, I get my strength and my grit from you." She explained how she wanted to get a tattoo of *my* sobriety date, to serve as a reminder that she can do anything without escaping and get through any challenge.

Hot tears began to stream down my face. I couldn't believe this beautiful, talented daughter of mine gave two shits about my quitting drinking. I mean, I knew she was proud of me. I knew she was glad to have a sober mom, but getting a tattoo of my sobriety date? I found it positively mind-blowing.

When I was her age, there would be no way I'd consider such a notion. I'd still be full of resentments from bygone years, not wisdom beyond my years. If the tables were turned and she was my mom, I'd probably get a tattoo of a hand flipping the bird, with the word "Mom" written on the middle finger. But here is this young lady who is forgiving and kind, who uses past experiences to fuel her future. She's got the secrets to life on lock. I was dumbfounded. I still am. A month later, we went together and got that tattoo, and it looks more beautiful on her than I ever could have imagined.

#SCRAPBOOK

Growing Up in the 80's...School Concerts, Girl Scout Cookies & Cabbage Patch Kids

From The Billy Graham Van,
Buses, Back of the Station Wagon,
Bakery, Barney Fife Campus Cop,
Beach Boardwalk, Bad Singing, &
Bagel Store ...to Bride

Ashley

Austin

Ava

2008-ish: 4 Kids
Ages 5 and Under...
Simultaneously
Brutal and
Wonderful

"Jen" & me & Shenanigans-
Before and After Getting
Sober ... BEFORE

AFTER

Just SOME of what I would've missed if I'd kept on drinking!

MORE of what I would've missed if I'd kept on drinking!

Annalise

Archer

Anders

72 Months–or 6 Years–
of Pregnancy…

Thank you to our wonderful friend "Dr. Nicholson" who delivered our 8 babies over 18 years!

The Sky's the Limit!
Grateful for our
Airline/Aviation Family

Seeing the World
Through
Sober Eyes...

Healed Relationships,
Healed Hearts,
Hope Restored!

EPILOGUE

AFTER ALL THOSE CONTRACTIONS, all that physical turmoil, after nine months of feeling totally outside of your body--the hormonal changes, the doubts and fears, the ridiculous guilt over normal things like eating processed lunch meat--you are handed that lovely, squishy, squirmy, fresh newborn. The world goes peculiarly quiet and everyone else is muted, clocks are paused and time stands still. You study the tiniest, most incredibly beautiful face you've ever imagined and lose your breath. A wave of untamed emotion rushes toward you, and you're powerless to stop it.

You watch as your entire being is transformed in an instant. You've never felt such desperate love, such defenseless exuberance for anything before, ever. It's so foreign and all-encompassing that you can't describe it. Maybe you're getting sewn up, surrounded by your partner, some nurses and your doctor—but you can't see them. Everyone else fades into the shadows and your heart floods and melts simultaneously as you cradle your own heartbeat in your arms and in a fraction of a second, you're transformed.

The same is true for getting sober. After all that struggle, after all that therapy, after all that internal work, you've wrestled with powerlessness. You've learned the heart of the serenity prayer, and you work on accepting the things you cannot change. You've found a God of your own understanding, or perhaps gone through a deconstruction and reconstruction of faith. You've taken a personal inventory and entrusted someone with the most intimate details you'd never dared to speak of before. In a variety of terrifying ways, you've cleared up the wreckage of your past. You have learned to strip off the old wallpaper of ideas, viewpoints and behaviors in exchange for new habits which actually serve you well and help you contribute positively to the stream of life. You're growing up, hitting the milestones. You learn to have awkward and difficult conversations that take courage beyond measure. You're becoming comfortable with being uncomfortable. And finally, you turn one.

On that first-year sobriety birthday, for one tear-filled moment, all the recovery friends laughing and hugging and surrounding you fade away and it's just you and the God of your understanding. You look down at the glow of that candle and it matches the internal glow you feel in your spirit. You stare in unbridled wonderment, that just 12 months ago you were a broken wreck, a vapor of a human. But in this moment, you get to blow out that candle with self-respect, without a single ounce of shame. Your heart overwhelmed with gratitude, you realize that in no way do you resemble who you used to be. That in fact, you've been reborn.

Suddenly, you realize the joy of being not only at the end of the first year, but actually on the precipice of your future.

At the time of this writing, I'm celebrating 10 years of sobriety. I can't believe it, but I also can. In some ways, it feels like I blinked, and here I am, and in other ways it feels like I climbed to the top of the Columbia Tower on the hottest summer day in Seattle with no A/C. I got here step by step, one effing growth opportunity at a time. I try to keep my sense of curiosity, joy and wonder, one day at a time. What I've invested comes back to me like a boomerang, but tenfold. Recovery continues to build on itself; and I remain *eternally expecting* to be amazed.

ACKNOWLEDGMENTS

Andrew: Mate, you're my rock, my best supporter, my biggest fan. Thank you for leaving Australia one last time 23 years ago and marrying me five whirlwind months later. Your selfless, action-oriented love speaks to me every day. Thank you for choosing to journey with me and watch me bloom, grow and change; I'm forever grateful. Thank you for sharing your own stirrings and growth with me. Thanks for plunging toilets, for loving the '80s as much as I do, for bringing me coffee every morning and for making me laugh like no one else. Thanks for giving me eight beautiful babies. You've been the best decision of my life, hands down. Thank you for being the systemic fuel that sustains our whole family. P.S. You're also my favorite husband.

 Ashley: Your grit and dedication astound and inspire me. The year you've just endured just shows off the Beast Mode that rumbles in your core, and I'm so proud of you. Your tat? Cue the tears. I can't even. You make me a better person. My love for you is an all-consuming treasure.

 Alex: You are smart as a whip and it's shocking how much you know at your age. Thank you for your willingness to help others; you're a patient and gifted teacher. Your caring heart and honest spirit move me. Who knew how that Servant's Heart award you earned in elementary school would stick so perfectly? I love ya and I think you hung the moon.

Austin: You're a kind, understanding and talented justice seeker. Your tomfoolery makes the world a better place. You are a great big brother and an inspiring and dedicated athlete. Your chilled-out manner always keeps me steady. I got nuthin' but big love for you.

Ava: You bring indescribable happiness to my heart. Truly, you're a better mother than I am. Your optimism and genuine joy are contagious. You're a fastidious student and gifted athlete. You light up a room and I want to be you when I grow up. Seriously. You're the Rory to my Lorelai. I love you endlessly.

Annalise: You're a firecracker who burst into my life and turned out to be the best surprise I've ever received. You're confident, decisive, full of life, honesty and love. I flippin' love and adore you.

Archer: You are sweet, sensitive and kind. You're a thinker and you ask great questions. You're patient beyond your years and the essence of quiet strength. I admire you and my heart explodes for you into a million pieces of love.

Anders: You are an adventure-seeker. You're funny, snuggly, loving and expressive. You are all-boy, with a sweetheart underneath. You crack me up and I'm just crazy about you. I love reading *Where the Wild Things Are* to you every night.

Audrina: You have a heart of gold and everything you touch becomes a warm, fuzzy blanket of hugs and kisses. You're a ray of glittery sunshine on a dark Seattle day. Who knew I had an Audrina-shaped hole in my heart? I can't even believe I got so ridiculously lucky to be your mom. Love you with exclamation points, arrows, bold print and X's and O's.

Mom, Dad, Weezy, Riri, the Cunos, Aunt Sherrie, Jan, Robin and the many Harrisons Down Under: Thank you so much for your love and support and commitment to family! XOXO

Mary F: Your wisdom and guidance have held the lantern as I walked through my darkness for the past decade. Your friendship, countless adventures and memories made are a bright spot in my life. Your open door, open heart, listening ear and wise counsel are all priceless to me. Words can never be enough.

Jayne S: Yaaaaas! Well Dorothy, we finally got our shit together...XOXO, Blanche. "Thank you for being a friend." But seriously you've been there for me the minute you saw me in my Britney Spears skirt. Just like Dionne Warwick, I know that "In good times, and bad times, you'll be on my side forever more..." Thanks for countless adventures of Bill and Bob, they are all just the best ever. Specifically, "Nudies Van," roadies, zip-tying the blue balls on unsuspecting peoples' trailer hitches and salty guacamole. PS) I don't know you but I love you! ;)

Kelli D: You're the "Champagne Singers" to my Lawrence Welk show and the animatronics to my blow-up Rudolph. Thanks for the unlimited supply of blow pops and Frescas in the Lady Sedan. I'm still pissed we didn't grab that chair off the side of the road in BFE. Thanks for journeying shoulder to shoulder with me as we trudge together and quote page numbers. #saved #simpatico

To my Wednesday Wolfpack: You guys are the best tribe, and we are so *not* a "glum lot." Like Madonna, I'm Crazy For You, and I'd do anything for you. Except go to another Res. 12 luncheon featuring an emotional acapella power ballad.

To BCS & VPG: I hope the spiritual questioning in this story isn't uncomfortable for you, but it was a crucial piece in my raw process of deconstruction of faith. Ultimately, that desperate questioning was the price of the liberating freedom I experience in my relationship with God today. Many thanks to Father Richard Rohr, whose teachings served as the foundation of my reconstruction. Oh! And I'm very sorry if I offended you with the handful of cuss words in my book. The authentic truth of my journey to hell and back had to come through. If I sell 74 million dollars' worth of books, I promise to buy us some new digs to make up for it. You are all family; I love you and am so grateful for you.

To the Inner Circle: You guys are all crazy-talented and you have inspired me beyond measure.

Anna D (and the Entire Launch Pad Gang): I can't thank you enough for teaching me how to make my book actually happen. I'd still be here with my book handwritten on binder paper sitting in a Trapper Keeper if it weren't for you. I'm *eternally grateful*.

Becky S: You are the Mr. Miyagi of editing. As you know, I'm unnaturally obsessed with you. Thanks for being cool about it when I inadvertently made you my therapist, not just my editor. (Why does that sound like a Hair Club for Men commercial? "Becky isn't just my editor! I'm her pro bono mental health client, too!") You'll have to pry my half of our matching necklaces from my cold, dead hand. Sorry not sorry.

Mitch N: Thank you so much for your dedication, kindness and friendship. Thanks for always taking my freak-out calls, for showing up and I'm so glad I never switched to Evergreen.

To my Strangely Assorted Crowd: Terry, John, Charles, Lisa and Patti: You're the best weirdos ever.

And that's the saddest effin' story I've ever heard. Me love you long time.

Jesse B & Matt W: You guys made the audiobook a dream come true! Thank you so much for your support, your friendship and all the laughs. Still hoping that playing Eddie Murphy's "Party All the Time" at maximum volume will drown out the neighborhood leaf blowers for next time.

Marisa B: Welp, I'm ever so grateful you weren't too weirded out when I accosted you at Mt. Hermon. So very thankful for your friendship and your talents. I love you so much and let's just say basically you are my Jesus-Guy handing out fast passes. PS May we never again be assaulted by "Cum on Feel the Noise" blasting uncontrollably after a long day of being bossed around at Disneyland by two five-year-olds.

Hope: You guys, 10 years, can you believe it?!?! It all started with you in the O.C. I'm forever grateful. Keep transforming lives!

To the God of My Understanding: My whole life, I made you so tiny, so small. I'm so sorry I failed to see that you required absolutely nothing from me. I had no idea that I could just let the poetry of the Bible wash over me, revealing the sweetest, easiest unconditional love from you with no hidden agendas. I'm living proof that you are far less rigid and therefore much bigger than the church ever taught. In the words of the Carpenters, "We've Only Just Begun."

Made in the USA
Las Vegas, NV
15 April 2021

21443418R00089